Wickwyn

Wickwyn

A Vision of the Future

Robert Van de Weyer

First published in Great Britain 1986
SPCK
Holy Trinity Church
Marylebone Road
London NW1 4DU

British Library Cataloguing in Publication Data
Van de Weyer, Robert
    Wickwyn
    1. Twentieth Century——Forecasts
    2. Twenty-first Century——Forecasts
    I. Title II. Society for Promoting Christian Knowledge
    303 4'9   CB161
    ISBN 0–281–04212–8

Printed in Great Britain by
Whitstable Litho Ltd, Whitstable, Kent

Contents

Introduction

It is a cliché – and yet true – to say that we live in a period of social and economic crisis. There is high and rising unemployment, with governments apparently unable to do anything to prevent it. After two centuries of rising prosperity, manufacturing industry in the Western world is facing rapid decline. The social welfare services are increasingly strained, starved of resources and yet faced with demands that grow heavier as each year passes. Politics is becoming more polarized, and yet ordinary people are losing faith in political solutions. Family life is increasingly hard to sustain, and the breakdown of families is becoming commonplace. And the Churches and other religious bodies find that their message of salvation seems to have little or no relevance to the problems people actually face.

This short book is about this crisis, and about the society that could emerge from it. It is written from the perspective of sometime in the mid-twenty-first century; so the last decades of the twentieth century are seen as one era – an important transitional era – in our history. And it is concerned with a particular village, Wickwyn, situated in central England; so events in Britain, and indeed in the world as a whole, are related to the evolution of a typical village community.

It is intended as a work of prophecy, in the Old Testament understanding of that word. It is simultaneously a prediction of what will happen, and a vision of what could happen if we had the moral courage to realize it. It is important that both aspects of prophecy are held together. Vision without prediction is likely to lead to Utopian fantasies which can never be realized. And prediction without vision ignores the role of human values and moral choices in shaping our future. Wickwyn in the twenty-first century is a village community which could actually evolve, and the majority of our population could live in such villages. It is a humane and peaceful way of life that people could realistically strive for, in which there would be both material prosperity and a high degree of spiritual fulfilment.

1

To explore the future one must understand the past, so the opening chapters are concerned with the history of Wickwyn from medieval times, through the industrial era of the nineteenth and twentieth centuries, until the present day – that is, until the middle of the twenty-first century.

1 Decline

The corporate village

The old Communion cup of the parish church, dated 1569, has inscribed on it 'The Towne of Wickwyne', and until the eighteenth century Wickwyn was like a small town, with a population of about 250 people, self-sufficient not only in food but in many of the other necessities of life: they provided their own entertainment, educated their children in the various skills needed for survival and cared for their own sick and elderly.

The medieval village was laid out along a single main street, with two smaller lanes going off to either side. The cramped cottages, made of timber and mud, were set in large gardens in which people grew their own vegetables, kept bees and looked after their own livestock. To the north and south were two vast open fields, each one over three hundred acres in size in which people had strips for cultivation: each year one field would be cultivated with wheat, barley and rye, while the other lay fallow. To the east, going down to the brook, was a large meadow, again divided into strips, from which hay was taken to feed the livestock in winter. In the centre of the village was the church, the house of God, a solid stone structure rising high above the flimsy houses of men; and beside it was the village green, where on summer evenings people met to drink ale and play sports, and where at the beginning of spring they danced round the maypole.

The villagers' cottages were not only places of rest and recreation, but also small factories. The women spun and wove wool into coarse cloth, and hemp and nettles into linen. The men tanned their own leather, and made the rough tools needed for cultivation. In the long winter evenings they carved the wooden spoons, plates and bowls they used at meal times, and made jugs and mugs from horn and leather. They peeled rushes for wicks, and made candles from beeswax. Shoe threads, halters, stirrup thongs, girths, bridles and rope were woven from hemp. The houses themselves were built by the inhabitants, and every man knew simple techniques of joinery, thatching and plastering. Wood for building, cooking and heating was gathered from the forest beyond the village. In addition, there were a small number of specialist craftsmen who augmented the cruder skills of ordinary folk: carpenters, blacksmiths, farriers, tinkers and shoemakers.

It was a tight, self-reliant community in which every face was familiar, and in which people met and chatted in the course of their daily occupation. Intermarriage meant that many people were related by blood, and family ties were strong. At haymaking, at harvest and when new houses were being built, people readily helped one another, and the material well-being of the village was the concern of all – to be celebrated annually at the harvest supper at the manor house. Those in authority, the lord of the manor and the parish priest, were treated with deference, and there were strict obligations binding on the peasant to work on particular days for the lord of the manor and to tithe part of his crop to the lord and the Church.

The Church herself was the symbol and guardian of the social order, and her doctrinal authority was undisputed. The individual was a Christian not by virtue of any personal commitment, but by being a member of the institutional Church, and knew God only through the Church's sacraments, administered by the priest. The strict hierarchical order of the Church, in which the individual was subsumed within the corporate institution, thus reflected the social order of the village and gave it divine sanction. People readily assumed that, however much they might have disliked it, an institutional Church so stable and unchanging must surely be the vehicle of the eternal will of God.

The dismembered village

To the people of Wickwyn, the Reformation of the sixteenth century was unexpected and seemingly unnecessary. Yet in fact it was the religious precursor of a profound social change which in the following centuries would break apart the corporate life of the village. The reformers taught that each individual stood in direct relationship to God, answering for themselves, and had no

4

need of Church, priests and sacraments to mediate. Thus there could be no ecclesiastical order upholding and guiding the social order, and there could be no binding obligation on the individual to conform to society's demands. Rather, each individual – guided by their own conscience and informed by the teaching of Scripture – must act according to their own will.

The Reformation had grown out of a new spirit of individual enterprise and free thinking which had swept Europe. There had been a rapid growth of trade in which individuals could accumulate fortunes through the buying and selling of goods, competing with one another in the market. Philosophers, scientists and artists asserted their own creative spirit, no longer willing to accept the ideas and beliefs of their ancestors, but pressing to make new discoveries and to give expression to new visions of their own. Even in those countries that remained loyal to the Church of Rome the same spirit took hold, and the Church itself adapted. In Wickwyn, and the tens of thousands of remote villages like it, the Reformation and the spirit behind it had little immediate impact, apart from on some of the religious rituals inside the church itself. The Mass in Latin became the Holy Communion in English, the coloured vestments of the priests were replaced by the monochrome of black cassock and white surplice, and the lavish murals telling the stories of the Bible and the saints were covered over by white limewash. Yet two centuries later a revolution occurred in Wickwyn that was caused by the same spirit of individualism that had inspired the reformers.

In 1786 the lord of the manor and the parish priest drew up a petition to present to Parliament to enclose the land within the village. They argued that if the land of the parish was owned privately, and landowners were not encumbered by ancient customs, new methods of cultivation could be applied and efficiency greatly improved. They were supported by the small number within Wickwyn who were free tenants of the lord, paying a money rent for the land they cultivated; the ordinary peasants, whose obligations to the lord were to do certain duties for him and hand over part of their crop, had no say. An act was passed, and the ownership of the land was divided mainly between the lord of the manor and the church, with the free tenants each receiving a small amount. The rest of the population received no land, and they lost their ancient right to cultivate strips and to take hay from the village meadow. Instead they had to seek employment from the landowners, receiving a wage with which to purchase what they needed. Those unable to find regular work were forced to depend on poor relief, provided by a small rate levied on the landowners.

In the decades following the enclosure, the face of Wickwyn altered beyond recognition. The large open fields were replaced by small fields. Much of the surrounding woodland was chopped down and brought under the plough, and areas of marsh were drained to provide yet more land for cultivation. Even the course of the brook was altered, its old meandering path replaced by a deep, straight channel less liable to flooding. New crops were introduced, and the animals were selectively bred to increase their size and yield. This revolution in agriculture was mirrored by an even greater revolution in manufacturing. The goods that had previously been made in peasants' cottages for their own use began to be produced in large factories in the expanding towns in the north of England. Thus a growing proportion of Wickwyn's agricultural output was sold to the city; and in return they bought their cloth, their tools and their household goods from the new factories.

In 1849 a railway was built passing only eight miles from Wickwyn, so it was possible for the first time for the ordinary tradesman or small farmer to travel the country. Outwardly, the life of an industrial city that they might visit was very different from that of a village like Wickwyn. The lines of smoke-blackened houses and the vast, noisy factories were in stark contrast to the small cottages and quiet fields of the countryside. The city dwellers themselves were nostalgic for village life, and in art and architecture the unchanging tranquillity of the lost medieval past continued to play on the urban imagination. The new churches in the cities were built in painstaking imitation of the gothic style of the village church, and the Anglo-Catholic movement which grew influential in the urban church was an attempt to revive the style of medieval worship.

But inwardly the lives of village and city were far closer than a superficial observer might have imagined, and village life became increasingly absorbed by the industrial economy. The breakdown of the close bonds within the village was writ large in the city, with individuals and families struggling on their own to survive and prosper. In the baptism, marriage and funeral registers of Wickwyn the great majority of menfolk in the nineteenth century were marked down simply as 'labourers'. The factory owner of the city referred to his employees as 'hands'. But in both the qualification was the same: a man was defined by the work he did for his employer. The wide range of crafts which the medieval peasants had automatically acquired in the course of their upbringing were rapidly forgotten, and men in the city and village were required only to perform repetitive tasks needing little thought or skill. The wide circle of relatives and friends within which people had lived and worked in the old village were shattered, as people moved across the country in search of work, and as they bought with cash the goods they needed. There remained an outward deference to those in authority, but this was more in fear of the power they wielded over their workers than in respect for their social position.

Despite the building of churches in the industrial cities, the bulk of the working population never attended them, and the colourful rituals were appreciated mainly by the richer classes. Working people who did attend church preferred the fervent hymn-singing of the independent evangelical chapels, their hearts warmed by praises to a saviour who reaches out in forgiving love to all who will receive him. In Wickwyn the parish church, which had traditionally been the spiritual heart of the community, found its congregation beginning to dwindle as the farm labourer, now reduced to the status of employee, no longer identified with the corporate life of the village. It thus became the church of the landowners who attended morning service, and of their servants who came to evensong, having prepared a cold meal for their masters. In 1862 an independent evangelical chapel was opened in Wickwyn, on a small plot of land fifty yards along the lane from the church. It was built simply in local brick, with arched windows and leaded lights as the only concesssion to decorative taste. Like its sister chapels in the city, it attracted the labourers, whose lusty singing on a Sunday evening could be heard outside in the village lane drowning the strained tones of the Anglican chants from the parish church. If there was to be popular religion in the age of individualism, it had to give to its adherents, for an hour or two

7

each week, the experience of warm fellowship, in contrast to the harsh soulless world in which they had to work.

Throughout the nineteenth century Wickwyn grew in prosperity, derived from the growing prosperity of the cities. Prices of farm produce remained high in relation to the cost of production, and the demand from the cities continued to expand. Agricultural wages rose, and the old wattle-and-daub houses were replaced by brick terraces in imitation of the dwellings of the industrial workers. At first the bricks and tiles were manufactured in a small works outside the village, using local clay, but by the end of the century it had become cheaper to buy building materials from the larger brickyards in the city of Peterthorpe, thirty miles away. It was, however, the landowners who enjoyed the greatest rise in income, and they were able to use their profits to buy shares in the growing industrial companies, so that an increasing proportion of their income was dividends derived from outside the village.

In 1870 the major landowner, the great grandson of the lord of the manor responsible for the enclosure of the parish, built for himself a huge new manor house on a low hill a mile outside the village. The house and the large garden around it were on a scale beyond the imagination of his medieval ancestors, and it required an army of chambermaids, footmen, cooks and gardeners, comprising almost one fifth of the population of Wickwyn, to serve the lord and his family in their new splendour. The style of the great house was gothic, in imitation of the fashionable architecture of the cities, which itself had grown out of a nostalgia for the medieval village. Yet imported back into the village it had nothing of the soft and simple beauty of the medieval parish church in the centre of Wickwyn, but was hard and graceless, punctuated by fussy decoration which was regarded as sophisticated. It was a symbol that the village had become a caricature of its past, with only the outward semblance of community life.

Thus, in a matter of three or four generations from the turn of the eighteenth century to the turn of the nineteenth, the social and economic life of Wickwyn was transformed. Until then it had been a close-knit community, each person with specific obligations and rights established by old tradition, and the village providing for almost all its material needs. Now the majority of the peasant population had neither rights nor obligations, but were dependent on employment and charity provided by the new landowners. And the village was one tiny part of an increasingly complex pattern of trade, dependent on the townspeople to buy their produce.

The death of the village

Throughout the nineteenth century there had been a steady trickle of young people moving out of Wickwyn in search of work in the cities. But, apart from the sadness of the families who often lost contact with their departing offspring, this had little effect on the life of the village. Rather, it prevented the population from rising and so eliminated potential unemployment. Yet the apparent stability of village life masked underlying forces of change which had been set in motion by the enclosures of the eighteenth century, and which in the twentieth century were to reduce the village to a tiny hamlet.

It was during the Great War and its aftermath that this final stage in Wickwyn's decline began to occur with dramatic speed. The young men who never returned from the war, and whose names were lovingly commemorated by a plaque on the north wall of the church, were the start of a fall in population which in two generations reduced Wickwyn from almost three hundred people to under fifty. The key to the change was the industrialization of farming itself. Until then, despite the new methods of cultivation and animal husbandry, farm work continued to be done mainly by hand. In 1917, as part of a wartime effort to boost food production, the first tractor was imported into Wickwyn from America. It could only pull a small plough, and so replaced animals rather than men; but soon it was superseded by machines which drove men off the land. Sixty years later the small enclosed fields had again been opened up, and the hedgerows cut down, to make way for huge, eight-wheeled, multi-plough tractors, aerial spraying of pesticides and herbicides, and vast mechanical harvesters. The old rotation of crops was abandoned in favour of continuous cereal production, with the new seed sown each autumn as soon as the old crop had been harvested, maintaining the fertility of the soil through ever more intensive use of fertilizers. Only nine people in the entire parish were required to cultivate its land, and their hands were more often covered with oil from the machines than soil from the fields.

Change in the twentieth century was no respecter of persons. Not only did the old peasant families move away to the factories in the cities, but the lord of the manor and the priest departed also. In the early 1950s the manor house was falling into ruins, the old squire, whose grandfather had built it, living in the east wing looked after by only an elderly butler and housekeeper. When he died his son, a chartered accountant in London, sold the estate to a life insurance company, who pulled down the house and rented the land in three large units to a new generation of business-minded farmers, trained at agricultural college. The church also found itself impoverished, caught between the falling value of its land rents and investments, and the rising cost of paying its clergy. The old rectory was sold in 1962, and the parish was served by a vicar living in a neighbouring village three miles away. The terraced cottages of the departing farm labourers, with their low ceilings and poky rooms, were left empty, and eventually demolished as unfit for human habitation.

By the late twentieth century all that remained of the old village were five substantial farm houses, two old pubs, the rectory and the church. The new farmers built themselves large houses with all modern conveniences, and for the handful of remaining labourers a terrace of council houses was constructed at the bottom end of the village. The pubs closed for lack of custom, and they and the old farmhouses were sold to affluent business men and professionals, who commuted each day to the nearby city of Peterthorpe, or beyond. They gutted the houses, rebuilding them from within to give the same modern comforts as the new farmers enjoyed, and yet striving to create the impression of antiquity by installing old fireplaces and beams.

In 1966 the independent chapel was closed and the elderly couple who had looked after it for almost forty years, and who were often the only attenders for Sunday worship, moved to an old people's home in Peterthorpe. In 1970 the village school was closed, its numbers having dwindled to only fifteen; the younger children were then taken by bus six miles to the nearest small town, while the older children went to a comprehensive school in Peterthorpe. The regular congregation at the parish church was only six, and the occasional coffee mornings to raise funds could not keep pace with the leaking gutters and crumbling plaster. Only at harvest festivals did the church fill with people, who decorated it with fruit and vegetables bought mainly from supermarkets in Peterthorpe. The church itself was now a ghostly caricature of its past.

Boom and bust

The three decades after the Second World War saw a prolonged economic boom throughout the Western world. It was a period of accelerated economic and cultural change which was both exhilarating and frightening. For two centuries previously economic development had been rapid and the Western world had become industrialized, and to each new generation the patterns of life in which their parents and grandparents had grown up were regarded as strange and alien: pictures and photographs of an earlier generation seemed to be of some foreign country. In the post-war boom the pace of change grew faster. It seemed that everything was subject to radical alteration, from the fixtures and fittings of the home to sexual morality, from the style of architecture to the pattern of worship in church. No tradition seemed sacred, and those who sought to uphold traditions were widely dismissed as merely reactionary. There was the hope that at last the conquest of nature was within human grasp, and that the problem of material scarcity could finally be resolved. And yet also there was a lurking sense that such burgeoning prosperity could not last, that a society so willing to pull up its roots even before they could become established would ultimately wither and die.

The first major sign that the boom could not be sustained was the massive inflation of the 1970s. Inflationary pressures had been building up throughout the boom within individual countries: groups of workers demanding ever higher wages; shareholders seeking ever higher profits; and governments seeking to boost their own expenditure to satisfy their electorates. These pressures led in turn to a rapidly-growing demand for natural resources, and so the world prices of raw materials began to rise steeply. The world economy seemed to burst in late 1973 when the mainly Arab producers of oil quintupled its price; and in the following years rates of inflation rose to heights previously unknown in Western countries. The immediate result of the Arab action on the affluent commuters of Wickwyn and elsewhere was a petrol shortage, which put them at the mercy of filling-station attendants. Yet after this, despite the impression of crisis, there was little short-term effect on people's lives. Salaries and wages rose in line with prices, and living standards remained high. The world's banks proved remarkably skilled at recycling the huge additional funds accumulated by the oil producers, making massive loans to developing countries to finance investment projects. This maintained world demand, and prevented an immediate slump which many had feared; but in the longer term it contributed to the much deeper crisis which followed.

Inflation can be regarded as institutionalized greed, in which the competing claims of children over their shares of the cake cause the price of the cake to rise. The symptom of the crisis which gripped the Western world from the 1980s to the early twenty-first century was unemployment, in which increasing numbers found themselves with almost no cake at all. Through the 1970s unemployment rose gradually, and went largely unremarked amidst the seemingly larger problem of inflation. After 1980 it grew rapidly worse, particularly in the old industrial cities, and defied all government attempts to cure it. By the late 1980s there were millions of people in the inner cities suffering severe poverty and deprivation which, although the social security system prevented actual hunger, was psychologically worse than that of earlier generations and indeed that of rural Africa and Asia. The old working-class communities, which had gradually become rooted in the inner cities since the Industrial Revolution, had been largely destroyed with the demolition of the old terrace houses and their replacement by huge local-authority estates. Thus the new unemployed found themselves isolated, imprisoned in flats which they could ill afford to heat or furnish, with only the private pleasure of the television to fill the day.

At first, for the people of Wickwyn unemployment was

merely an item on the television news, with pictures of large factories in the northern cities being closed. The prices of farm products remained high, due mainly to financial support from the EEC, so that farmers were initially immune from the devastation of manufacturing industry. The firms in Peterthorpe were mainly producing light consumer products, and for a period, while those with jobs remained affluent, demand for these goods remained buoyant; so the commuters in Wickwyn employed in Peterthorpe continued to feel secure and confident. The few in Wickwyn who worked in the public sector – a teacher, a doctor, a civil servant and a social worker – were also initially unscathed, as public expenditure was maintained at a high level: despite cries of anger and even strikes in opposition to government policy, the expenditure cuts in the public sector in the 1980s were still trivial compared with what was to follow.

But then in 1990, within a few weeks of each other, two of the commuters of Wickwyn put their houses on the market and shortly afterwards left the village. The increasing unemployment in the country as a whole, and in other parts of the Western world, was now depressing demand for consumer products, and so firms in Peterthorpe were being forced to make large numbers of their employees redundant. By 1995 three other commuters had left also. Cuts in the public sector were becoming increasingly savage, and the social worker and the civil servant were made redundant, while the teacher was offered early retirement at the age of 49. House prices in Wickwyn and other villages began to fall sharply, and the old farmhouses extensively renovated a few decades earlier were reverting to their former shabbiness.

Farms, too, began to suffer. A declining economy led to declining demand for the more expensive foods, especially meat; and this in turn depressed the price not only of livestock but also of cereals, most of which were used to feed animals. The efforts of governments to maintain artificially high prices for agricultural products to protect farmers proved impossibly expensive, and were politically untenable in the light of mass unemployment in the cities. So farmers' incomes and land prices fell, the large machinery was too costly to run and replace, and the large inputs of artificial fertilizers and pesticides were too expensive. The squeeze on the tenant farmers was also felt by the landowners, the investors and the life assurance companies in London, who found their land revenues falling. Thus Wickwyn, having become wholly subsumed in the national and international economy following the enclosures of the eighteenth century, was now sharing that economy's suffering.

2 Crisis

The technological revolution

When unemployment had begun to rise sharply in the early 1980s people spoke of the Western world as suffering a 'recession', hoping that like all previous recessions it would soon come to an end, with demand for goods and services recovering and the number of jobs rising. This pattern of recession followed by recovery and boom had occurred many times since the Industrial Revolution. But, despite intermittent signs of recovery, unemployment continued to rise through the late twentieth century and into the following century. Western countries, and indeed the world as a whole, were entering a period of transition in which social and economic life was being radically changed.

Through the last decades of the twentieth century the major cause of rising unemployment was the remorseless shift of manufacturing industry away from Europe and North America to Asia and Latin America. This process was accelerated by the success of the Western banks in recycling the huge revenues of the oil producers in the 1970s into investment projects in the developing countries. More importantly, the major multinational manufacturing firms shifted their plants to countries where wages were low and the work-force well disciplined – or 'docile', as Western trade unionists would have it. Within a few short years the activities of the multinational companies achieved greater transfers of resources to the hitherto poor countries than had been achieved by decades of development aid from Western governments and charities. For a period in the late 1980s high world interest rates created a financial dilemma as the developing countries were unable to service their debts. But in fact these debts were no greater as a proportion of national income than those America and other Western countries had incurred in the nineteenth century at a similar stage of industrial development.

In the nineteenth century the industrialization of the West caused the destruction of the traditional craft industries of Asia and Africa. As Gandhi had protested, cheap Lancashire cotton flooding into India had destroyed India's old economy and impoverished her people. Now industrialization in India and elsewhere was flooding the Western world with cheap goods, and destroying the great manufacturing enterprises that had dominated the world. In 1950 less than one twentieth of the consumer goods purchased in Britain were imported; by the late 1980s over half were imported, and the proportion continued to grow. In 1950 half the working population in Britain had been directly employed in the manufacturing industries, and millions of others had been in service industries related to manufacturing; by the early 1980s only a quarter were employed in the manufacturing industries, and the proportion continued to fall. For the first time in history Britain, once the workshop of the world, began to import more manufactured goods than she exported.

Yet throughout the late twentieth century another force was at work which ultimately proved far more important than the geographical shift in industry. The technology which had developed since the Industrial Revolution had been essentially simple and mechanical in its functions, able to perform straightforward tasks at great speed. But, although it frequently replaced manual work, it always required human operators needing little or no skill. So technical progress actually absorbed labour in the expanding industries, and the unskilled nature of the work meant that people could readily move from agriculture and the old craft industries to the new factory production lines. Now, however, the development of cheap microelectronic intelligence fundamentally changed the nature of machinery, replacing mental as well as manual work, and permanently displacing human labour. To begin with its main application was in information processing, replacing filing cabinets and typing pools in the office. But the use of microelectronic aids to design, and micro-electronic control of machines for manufacturing goods – the development of robots – enabled factories to run with greatly reduced work-forces. And the people that were still required were not unskilled operatives, but highly-trained engineers and designers.

Then in the twenty-first century came a no less radical development in the materials needed for manufacturing. From earliest history mankind had harnessed and used the materials which nature provided: stone, timber, metal and, more recently, fossil fuels such as coal and oil. Industrial expansion led to fears that the stock of such materials was being depleted so quickly that shortages would soon seriously threaten the world economy. Now scientific research into the structures of materials, which had been quietly in progress in the twentieth century, enabled firms to synthesize materials precisely for the purposes required. This meant both that far fewer natural resources were required, and that there was far greater flexibility in the way basic resources were used. Thus the shortages that people had feared never occurred, and at the same time many of the primary producers of raw materials found themselves superseded, their work-forces diminishing along with those in the old manufacturing industries.

The revolution in technology was as profound and far-reaching in its effects as the Industrial Revolution had been. The Industrial Revolution had changed the organization of production, initially by gathering workers into factories with each worker doing one small, simple task repetitively in a production line, and then by introducing large-scale machinery to take over many of these simple tasks. Now production itself had been revolutionized: through scientific analysis humankind had become able to simulate both its own intelligence and the processes of nature. The technological revolution was no respecter of countries and regions: not only did it hasten the rise of unemployment in the West, but it undermined the supremacy of the newly-emerging countries. All alike found themselves in the same dilemma: on the one hand new technology offered the prospect of high living standards for all humanity; on the other hand a growing proportion of humankind found itself useless and redundant, unable to share in the production or the enjoyment of this prosperity. The physical and social structure in which people lived incarcerated them. Large cities, developed to house the work-forces of large factories, now had no purpose or reason for existence, but simply confined people in helpless passivity. A society which for over two centuries had been based on work for money, and in which

17

people had organized their lives in accordance with their paid occupation, was now as redundant as many of its members.

Crisis in the body politic

In a nightmare there is sometimes a strange and terrifying paralysis, when one is aware that some horrible event is about to occur and yet one is incapable of moving to prevent it. The situation of Western societies of the late twentieth century had a similar nightmarish quality: there was visibly vital work to be done in satisfying many basic needs, and yet people found themselves paralysed, unable to do the work required. There were children and young people to be educated; yet the schools were becoming steadily more deprived of teachers and resources. There were the sick and old to be cared for; yet the health services became more impoverished and the queues of needy patients longer. Houses were growing shabby and the numbers of homeless and those living in slums increased; yet the construction industry was starved of work, and bricklayers and carpenters idle. People were cold, unable to pay for sufficient heating in their homes; yet all sorts of technologies for harnessing the environment's energy lay unexploited and undeveloped. And families, though not hungry, were malnourished, subsisting on processed foods bought in supermarkets, without land to cultivate their own food; yet agriculture was depressed, the number employed in the fields negligible, and the industrialized methods of cultivation were destroying the fertility of the land.

At first people resorted to old and time-worn political ideologies in their search for solutions, taking these ideologies to their logical extremes; and for a period the political divide between Right and Left grew deeper. The Left urged greater public expenditure on welfare, to absorb some of the unemployed in public services and to pay the remainder generous benefits. The Right urged reduced public expenditure and taxation, believing that firms operating in the free market without government interference would prosper and expand in such a way as to boost employment. As the crisis of unemployment and the accompanying deprivation grew more acute, so political con-

18

flict became more bitter, with peoples' minds closed to rational debate by the anxiety and anguish of the crisis. But the nature of the crisis defied both the old ideologies.

Rising unemployment initially forced greater public expenditure to provide additional benefit payments. The left-wing policy of further increases in public expenditure had to be financed, in part at least, by adding to the burden of taxation on those in the private sector producing goods and services for the market. Already at the beginning of the 1980s almost half of all income and expenditure was being taken in taxation. The left-wing policy increased this proportion steeply, which in turn discouraged private enterprise and investment, and thus a vicious circle was created. The rising level of taxation only hastened the decline in the number of those employed in the private sector, which meant that even higher rates of taxation had to be levied on those who remained in private employment – so adding a further twist to the downward spiral.

The right-wing policy, however, offered no better prospect. The only way to prevent taxation from rising was to respond to the increasing expenditure on unemployment benefit by cutting back on other forms of public expenditure. And if taxation was actually to be reduced, the public expenditure cuts had to be even larger. Yet these cuts themselves threw many of those in the public sector out of work, thus adding to the expense of unemployment benefit much of what had been saved by the cuts themselves. So this policy also created a vicious circle. Preventing taxation from rising implied ever larger cuts in public spending, which caused more unemployment and more payments of benefits – to be financed by further public expenditure cuts.

In practice, despite the bitterness of their rhetoric, governments of either persuasion had little real control, and both were forced into a similar compromise. Left-wing governments soon found that steeply-rising taxation was politically unacceptable, as well as economically disastrous. The alternative ways of financing public expenditure, by borrowing or by printing new money, were also impossible to sustain. As the American experience in the early 1980s showed, of financing huge public expenditure by borrowing, interest rates were forced up to attract the necessary loans and private investment severely damaged. And, as profligate governments since the Roman

19

Empire have found, creating new money debased the value of money through inflation. Thus, ambitious plans to expand public expenditure soon had to be abandoned. Similarly, right-wing governments quickly found that promises of reducing taxation could not be kept in the face of rising unemployment; and even to prevent taxation from rising meant increasingly severe cuts in public expenditure.

So throughout the late twentieth and early twenty-first centuries, governments of all sides were trapped in an impossible dilemma. Whatever their wishes, rates of taxation tended to rise, both because benefits for the growing numbers of unemployed people had to be financed, and because the number of people in the private sector able to pay tax was diminishing. At the same time, public expenditure on health care, education, roads and the whole range of goods and services provided by the State was cut ever more deeply; and the level of benefit paid to the unemployed gradually fell, making their deprivation ever more acute.

The poor thus became poorer, and the gap between them and those who continued to have well-paid jobs – and who could afford to buy private health care and education – became wider. Initially the most vulnerable groups were unskilled manual workers, whose jobs in manufacturing industry disappeared, and young people, since firms faced with the need to reduce their labour force typically did not recruit new workers to replace those who retired. But by the 1990s almost every class in society found itself at risk. Industrial decline meant fewer managers and workers with traditional engineering skills were needed. The private service industries began to suffer too: shops and restaurants found custom dwindling, and even banking and other financial services, which had become major employers, found that economic decline combined with the introduction of information technology drastically reduced their work-forces, while the financial starvation of the public sector meant that teachers, nurses, doctors and all involved in the welfare services were also in danger of redundancy.

Crisis in the human spirit

The popular music of the 1950s and early 1960s sang the praises of affluence and prosperity: romantic love was bound up with

20

the possession of fast cars, transistor radios, and clothes in the latest fashion. Since the Industrial Revolution the compensation for the impersonal, mindless work in which the majority of people had been engaged was the promise of ever-growing material rewards – 'commodity fetishism' as Karl Marx described it. In the mid-twentieth century the promise was being fulfilled not only for the upper and middle classes, the descendants of the landowners, but also for the descendants of the old peasantry.

Yet by the late 1960s the popular music of the post-war generation was already urging escape from this prosperity: even at the moment of its realization the promise was proving worthless. As social philosophers of the nineteenth century such as Weber and Durkheim had predicted, the inner spiritual logic of continuous industrial growth led to disillusionment and despair, because people were denied the sense of corporate solidarity and shared values which gave meaning and purpose to their activities. The new popular heroes were rock stars who appeared to have freed themselves from all moral and material disciplines, and who urged retreat to the hippy commune where love was free, where prosperity was replaced by the more direct pleasures of hashish and 'acid', and where authority had been abolished. Even in Wickwyn teenagers sang the praises of the flower people of San Francisco, dedicated to the simple virtues of peace and love. And those whose parents provided sufficient pocket money would discreetly share joints of hashish at little parties in their bedrooms, disguising the smell from their parents with incense and joss-sticks.

Then in the late 1970s and early 1980s, as the economy began to reject individuals by denying them work, a new spirit of violence found expression in music: 'I like the sound of breaking glass', as one hit record droned in a dull, rhythmic monotone. The punk heroes who replaced the stars of the hippy movement were brash and raw, urging escape through the destruction of the public signs of affluence. Finally there ceased to be a popular culture in which the mass of young people participated, and the young split into diverse small groups, each with its own style of clothes, music and behaviour. Being denied work and status by society, young people devoted their energies to creating elaborate forms of dress, developing dances which required great skill and athleticism, and making their own styles of music. Just as religious groups throughout history had created and asserted their corporate identity through rituals requiring precise conformity in appearance and action, so groups of young people gave themselves a sense of community by the same means. For some groups violence was part of their way of achieving solidarity, and the terraces of football clubs and the shopping arcades of the city centres occasionally became scenes of brutal gang warfare. But most groups were docile and peaceful towards outsiders, preferring the security of their own companionship.

Yet, despite the identity they found in their sectarian groups, the shadow of despair and depression hung over the lives of young people who had never known purposeful employment; and as the generation who reached maturity in the 1980s grew towards middle age at the end of the century, and as further generations shared their hopeless fate, so the shadow grew darker. They depended on State benefits for the necessities of life, and had no material purpose beyond living from one social security cheque to the next. Hundreds and thousands became dependent on drugs. Illegal drug-taking, a headline catcher in the optimistic days of the 1960s, was so common that it was no longer a topic of outrage or even comment. And legal drugs for mental distress, prescribed by doctors, became a comfort on which growing millions depended; in effect the medical profession became the unwitting agent of social control, dispensing drugs for depression which made the economic circumstances which caused the depression more easy to accept without protest. Thus, like the idle poor of ancient Rome who were kept quiet by the provision of free bread and circuses by the Emperor, the unemployed of late twentieth-century Britain were maintained in passive acquiescence by State benefits and drugs.

In unconscious reflection of the quasi-religious solidarity of the groups of unemployed young, those with jobs began to attend church in larger numbers; and after two centuries of decline, to the surprise of the clergy, congregations started to grow. The despair of the unemployed was echoed in the anxiety of those in work, who were acutely aware of the vulnerability of

22

their own economic advantage. The most spectacular growth was amongst the evangelical churches, whose message one-and-a-half centuries earlier had appealed so strongly to the impoverished industrial workers: for them it had offered the promise of eternal spiritual bliss after a lifetime of material deprivation; for the converts of the late twentieth century it offered the security that God, through his Holy Spirit, would guide and provide for them in an insecure world. But the more staid, less intense churches also experienced steady, if unspectacular, growth in numbers, providing a somewhat different means of responding to people's anxiety. On the one hand, they offered a vehicle by which, in prayer and in deeply-felt statements of concern, people could express their anguish at the suffering of those less fortunate. On the other hand, in their undemanding fellowship and in the unchanging rhythm of their worship, they gave people a sense of emotional stability, not offering any divine solutions but rather enabling them to confront more honestly the potential instability of their material lives. Unlike the aristocracy of old, who felt secure in their privilege, and for whom church worship affirmed their sense of divine approval of the social order, those attending church now were only too conscious of how fragile and uncertain was the employment on which their privilege rested; and for many the church offered the spiritual means by which to live with that uncertainty.

Thus Western society found itself caught in two profound contradictions. At the material level, at the very moment when new technology offered the means of winning mankind's age-old battle against scarcity and deprivation, people were unable to organize themselves to use this technology to their mutual benefit. The folly of the Western world's economic and political structures negated the genius of her scientific and technological insights. At the spiritual level, when people potentially could have broken free from the alienating and impersonal way of life forced upon them by industrial growth, they were unable within the context of the old industrial cities to recreate a more shared, personal way of life in co-operation with others. The quasi-religious groups of the unemployed young, and the growing church congregations of those in employment, were expressions of people's yearning for community. But it was only when this yearning bore fruit in a new way of life, involving the reorganization of daily life and work, that the resolution of these contradictions was found.

Movement to the countryside

In past centuries there have been large shifts of population within countries, and indeed between countries. Since the sixteenth century whole continents – North and South America and Australasia – have been populated by immigrants, mainly from Europe, overwhelming the indigenous people. Britain itself is a complex mixture of ethnic groups originating from throughout Europe and beyond, and the early settlements which developed into medieval village communities were made up of people pushing outwards into previously uninhabited terrain. The Industrial Revolution of the late eighteenth and early nineteenth centuries sucked people from villages throughout the country into the new cities in the north of England. And the development of engineering and light industries in the late nineteenth and early twentieth centuries drew people to the Midlands and the south-east. Changing economic circumstances have throughout mankind's history caused movements of population.

Government policy in the latter half of the twentieth century sought to inhibit further spontaneous movement. Planning laws enacted in the 1940s, designed to maintain good order in the use of land, in effect confined the majority of the population to the cities. Wickwyn and numerous villages like it, having declined to tiny hamlets, were not allowed to grow; a few villages, designated for development by the planners, were allowed to sprawl and become small new towns. Rather than allow the unemployed to move, the government sought throughout the 1960s and 1970s to bring work into the areas of the country where the old heavy industries were declining, by subsidizing new firms to set up there. In relation to the money spent the results were poor: gaily-painted signs on the roads into decaying northern towns, advertising free new factory sites, grew dirty and tatty as the sites remained largely unfilled. Where these regional policies were comparatively successful, the economic decline of

an area was temporarily delayed; but this success was at the
expense of other areas which the new firms had rejected. Thus
the main effect of the policy was to shift rather than to lift the
burden of unemployment.

At root, the failure of the government's regional policies was
because the industrial city itself was now redundant. The conur-
bations had come into being to serve the factories where large-
scale production required hundreds or even thousands of men
at a single place of work. The factory owners themselves had
often built street upon street of terraces to house the labourers
drawn from the countryside. No one ever imagined it was
humane and desirable to live in such massive, concentrated
groups; but economic necessity compelled it. After the Second
World War local governments tried to make mass housing more
pleasant by replacing the old terraces with blocks of flats; but
the main effect was simply to damage the fragile networks of
human relationships which had developed within the terraced
streets. Now, however, the disappearance of the large manufacturing plants meant that people no longer needed to live in such
cities; and unemployment turned the cities into prisons of enforced idleness.

So in the last years of the twentieth century a growing number
of people of all social classes began to explore new ways of living
and new forms of work away from the city. Those made redundant in middle age, with little chance of finding another full-
time job, wanted to use their assets to purchase property in the
countryside, where there would be space to provide food and
other goods for themselves, and in some cases to start small
businesses. Others, still in work, sought to reduce their working
hours to follow a similar course, combining part-time employment with a greater amount of time working at home. Many
young unemployed people were too depressed and demoralized, and too well established in a life of idleness, to consider
such a change; but some were prepared to accept considerable
discomfort and hard work to build a new life for themselves in
strange surroundings.

There was thus a growing movement from the cities and
suburbs into the villages. In the face of this pressure, and realiz-
ing that the prospect of new building in the countryside and the
expansion of small-scale rural industry offered hope for new

employment, the government gradually relaxed the planning regulations, freeing people to move as they wished. The price of agricultural land had already fallen, due to the decline in farm revenue, and the relaxation of the planning laws meant that the high prices for building plots in villages, caused artificially by the planners making such plots so scarce, were now eliminated. So land for agriculture and building alike was relatively cheap, and people of quite modest means could purchase land on which to establish a new home. Thus the population of Wickwyn, in common with tens of thousands of other villages like it, started to expand, continuing over the following decades until today, when it stands at almost nine hundred people. The first newcomers were pioneers, creating by trial and error a way of life quite different from that of the industrial city. But once the trend had become set, so less courageous souls could follow their example. To begin with, the newly-arriving couples would mostly live in caravans and mobile homes while they set about building their houses. So at first, what had previously been a quiet and pretty – although almost dead – village seemed noisy and ugly. But now it has become relatively stable and peaceful, its new buildings gradually weathering, and new trees and hedges growing to maturity.

Without conscious intention, but simply in response to people's demands, the layout of the modern village of Wickwyn is similar to that of its medieval predecessor. In the centre stands the old church, and to its south the parish council has purchased eight acres which has become the village green: it is used for football and cricket, and for festivals; and on the side adjoining the churchyard is a flower garden with chairs and tables, and a cafeteria open in the summer months. The old independent chapel to the north-west of the church has been refurbished as the village hall, with a stage where a three-decker pulpit once stood. Beyond the chapel is the crossroads, at which the four main roads through the village meet; in addition a network of lanes has been built running from these roads, so the village now occupies about 250 acres. Most houses stand in about a quarter of an acre, running in a strip from the lane; the land used mainly for intensive cultivation but leaving room for a small lawn and a garden. To the south-east of the church, looking on to the village green, is a small health clinic and hospital, and a school used by children during the day and for adult classes in the evenings. Further round the green are the newly-established shops and a pub; another pub, the Three Horseshoes, has been re-opened in its original seventeenth-century building at the crossroads. To the west of the village, where once stood the gibbet on which criminals were hanged, is a modern factory, part of a large multinational company making vehicles.

Life in the cities has undergone a complementary change. The medieval city was comparatively small, and functioned as a commercial and cultural centre serving the majority of the population who lived in the rural areas. It had thriving markets where the farmers and the cottage craftsmen could come in from the villages to sell their produce. And some, like Peterthorpe, had magnificent cathedrals, whose structure incorporated the most exquisite stone carvings, whose walls were festooned with gloriously colourful paintings, and where religious dramas were performed and religious festivals celebrated with lavish splendour. In the industrial age of the nineteenth and twentieth centuries the balance shifted, the cities expanding to become the centres of production, and the villages serving them. Peterthorpe's growth was stimulated by the advent of the railway, when it became a major junction, which in turn attracted new industry. After the Second World War it expanded further when it was chosen for development, with new townships and industrial estates built round it, trebling its land area. Just over three-quarters of a century after their construction, those houses, many of which had already become shabby and were nearing the end of their life, were demolished, along with some of the suburbs built in the 1930s.

Peterthorpe has again reverted to being a commercial and cultural centre, serving a population living in large villages in the surrounding area. The old cathedral continues to dominate, and near it is a thriving shopping area, with a few large department stores but mainly consisting of smaller specialist shops offering a wider range of goods than can be stocked in the village shops. The theatre and concert hall built in the 1960s have far larger audiences than they enjoyed when they first opened, because people from the countryside frequently mark special occasions by a trip into the city to see a live professional performance. The large general hospital, also built in the 1960s, continues to flourish, treating illnesses beyond the competence of the village clinics. More recently, a small university has been established, using the sturdy old buildings once used by a company making diesel engines. On the outskirts of the city there remain some factories and, more significantly, the management and research headquarters of five large manufacturing firms which have plants around the country and abroad.

In many respects the pattern of life has returned to that of the medieval past. A typical village such as Wickwyn is no longer a quiet dormitory for commuters but a place of work, its population being about ten times its number in the mid-twentieth century. In the nation as a whole the majority of the population now live in large villages, most of which are much bigger than they were in medieval times to accommodate the greater population. As in the medieval village, there is a high degree of self-reliance, with families and small-scale industries providing much of what they need.

Yet both materially and spiritually the life of modern Wickwyn is profoundly different from the past. The medieval economy was labour-intensive, but inefficient and unproductive in its use of time. People helped and supported one another in their daily work, but the community was inward-looking with little knowledge of life beyond the parish boundary. The industrial economy which followed became highly capital-intensive, but careless and wasteful in its use of the earth's resources, and ultimately wasteful of human labour. In an era of mass markets and mass communications people throughout the world were economically dependent on one another; yet there was little sense of belonging to a community in which people knew and cared for one another personally. The modern economy is again labour-intensive, but human activity is now harnessed to equipment and methods of production which are efficient in their use of both labour and resources. The individual is rooted in the community where economic relationships are personal, and where a sense of corporate identity is fostered by the pattern of daily work; and yet the village is economically and culturally open, in constant communication with places and people beyond the parish.

The modern lifestyle thus has a mixture of features from both the medieval and the industrial age, and yet is a radical development from both. This has profound implications for every aspect of human society: family life; welfare – the way in which society cares for the young, the sick and the old; politics – the ways in which decisions affecting society as a whole are made; and also for religious life.

3 Family

The erosion of the family

The process of industrialization in the nineteenth and twentieth centuries had gradually eroded the life of the family. The medieval family had been an extended network of relatives living within the village or its neighbouring parishes. Members of the family worked together in providing for their material needs, within the home itself or in the fields nearby. But in the mid-twentieth century most families consisted of a married couple and their children, living independently and seeing their relatives only occasionally on social visits. For husbands, and increasingly for wives also, their daily work took them outside the home and neighbourhood into large factories and offices. Thus the family home was reduced to a place of rest and relaxation.

Yet, more than ever, the family came to be regarded as the primary source of spiritual and emotional fulfilment. The factories and the offices were generally soulless places in which employees had little personal involvement either with fellow workers or with the goods or services they were engaged in producing. Division of labour, with each person specializing in a single task, meant that much of their work was dull and monotonous; and the sheer size of the factory or office meant that relations between worker and manager were often antagonistic, with the individual unable to identify their own well-being with that of the organization as a whole. The family grew in emotional importance as the primary, and for many people the only, source of companionship and love. Marriage was held in higher esteem than ever, and people longed to find the perfect partnership which would yield total emotional and sexual fulfilment. Romantic love leading to lifelong union was idealized in countless popular songs, the same vision appealing to each new generation with only the style of music changing. The marital home and its furnishings became the focus of the deepest concern, and couples would struggle to save money and devote

an area was temporarily delayed; but this success was at the
much of their spare time in order to beautify their houses. In the
nineteenth century in the industrial cities, there was a flowering
of clubs and societies in which neighbours met regularly after
work to pursue common interests and sports, recreating something of the communal atmosphere of the village from which
they or their parents had emigrated. But in the twentieth century even these largely died out as the quest for home improve-
ments, as well as record players, televisions and video recorders,
kept people within their own homes when work had finished.

The churches came to see their main social and moral role as
being guardians of the ideal of perfect marriage and harmonious
family life. They had largely withdrawn from wider political and
social concerns, and the maintenance and encouragement of
family bonds became their overriding interest. Deviation from
this ideal was thus strongly condemned. Not only did divorce
and homosexuality incur moral reprimand, but celibacy – the
way of life chosen by the Church's own founder – was regarded
with suspicion; and some churches and dioceses even refused,
as a matter of policy, to have celibate priests and ministers.

Yet in people's attitudes to the family there was a profound
contradiction. The nuclear family as it had evolved in industrial
society was simply unable to fulfil the hopes placed in it. The
very forces which had led people to expect so much out of
family life were the same forces which had eroded family life,
and now prevented it from satisfying those expectations. While
the ideal of marriage was held in such high esteem, actual
marriages were increasingly prone to break down amidst bitterness and disillusionment. Since their daily work drew them
apart, each to a separate factory or office, couples had few areas
of shared interest and concern. Yet after work they found themselves alone together within their home. There was thus an
enforced emotional closeness, yet with little opportunity for
daily companionship. This often caused marriages to become
set in a pattern of mutual possessiveness and resentment,
with a desire to be fully involved with one's partner, and yet
with a sense of being imprisoned by that involvement. The
marital home became for many a place of loneliness, anger and
depression.

The erosion of the family in industrial society led to a growing
obsession with physical sex. Advertisers frequently used erotic

imagery to market products which had no direct connection with sex: they intuitively understood that, in a society which offered little emotional fulfilment, sexual feelings would become separated from human love, and thus be readily associated with the purely physical pleasure of a material product. The ideal of a loving, faithful marriage was being constantly undermined by an attitude to physical sex which made promiscuity seem quite natural and acceptable. The frequent failure to find perfect love within marriage only accentuated this attitude, leading people to seek through sexual adventure a substitute for what they could not find in a faithful partnership. Homosexuals, too, found themselves caught in a similar confusion of sexual attitudes. While homosexual love remained widely disapproved of, it was accepted that in practice homosexuals were not only sexually active, but in constant search of new sexual partners. Only celibacy continued to be regarded as abnormal and as a sign of psychological and physical failure.

By the late twentieth century the break-up of marriages had become commonplace, and no longer a cause of scandal or even comment. Although most people continued to marry, there was growing ambivalence amongst young people towards the institution of marriage: whilst the ideal of romantic love and lifelong partnership continued to appeal, observation of their parents' marriages led to a justifiable suspicion and caution. It became increasingly acceptable to change partners during the course of life; and after one marriage and divorce, many people ceased to bother with a marriage commitment.

The active home

The families which have moved to Wickwyn have found both the material and the emotional aspects of their life together undergoing profound change, bringing couples closer together in their daily occupations, and yet making them less dependent on one another for companionship and love.

The most immediate change for couples arriving in Wickwyn is the expansion of shared activities within the family: the building and maintenance of the home; the cultivation and processing of food; and meeting one's own energy requirements. This

32

in turn means that the newcomer must acquire the skills needed for this more self-reliant way of life. The wide range of skills which the medieval villager learnt during his upbringing had long since been forgotten, and now an equally wide range of new skills is needed. Happily, like those of the medieval village the skills and techniques needed are mostly quite straightforward, and can be learned through practice rather than through formal education. This is because modern technology enables the manufacture of tools and materials which are comparatively simple to use, so that even such tasks as plumbing and plastering no longer require expert craftsmanship. Moreover, people in such a small community readily give support and advice, passing on to newcomers what they have learnt, and helping one another in major tasks.

The first priority for most newcomers who have purchased a site is the building of their home. This is constructed not only to accommodate the family but also to supply and save much of the energy it needs. The typical house is simple in appearance but sophisticated in design, so as to make maximum use of the heat of the sun. It is long and thin, the width of a single room, running from east to west, with large windows facing south and almost no windows on the other walls. Thus, even on cold, bright days in mid-winter the direct sunlight provides much of the heat required. The partitions between rooms within the house are thick brick walls, and the floors are covered in quarry tiles, which together on sunny days store the heat pouring in from the windows, reducing the room temperature during the day and releasing the heat in the evening. To prevent the houses from overheating on hot summer days, the large, south-facing windows can be slid back so that the rooms open directly onto the garden; and shades can be pulled out to shield the rooms from direct sunlight. The exterior walls are made of an outer leaf of local brick, with a wide cavity filled with insulating material, and an inner leaf of thermal block; the windows are double-glazed with a form of glass that releases little heat from inside; and beneath the floor and above the ceiling there are more thick layers of insulating material. Thus the combined effect of natural heating from the sun and a high degree of insulation means that the requirement for additional heating is a fraction of what was needed in houses built in the twentieth century and before.

Running along the south side of the house is a simple paved terrace, on the south edge of which is what appears to be a raised flower-bed built of brick, about two feet high and four feet wide. Herbs and decorative flowers are grown round the edge, and in the middle there are a series of solar collectors. Even on dull days the water within them is heated significantly by the warmth of the sun, and through the natural process of warm water rising it flows into a tank in the roof space – it is thus a simpler system, with no need for a complex system of valves, than the original solar panels which people used to put on top of the roof. There is also a small windmill to generate electricity, which feeds directly into an immersion heater to warm the water still further. The house is heated by underfloor pipes and, since the surface area to be warmed is so great, the water running through the pipes need not be very hot; so usually the heating from the solar collectors and the windmill is sufficient, and only on dark winter days is additional heating needed from mains electricity.

The rooms are generous in size; since the major cost of building is the time taken in construction, and since the family itself does most of this work, it can afford to give itself ample space. The biggest room is the kitchen at one end of the house, which is fitted with a wide range of electrical equipment for the processing and cooking of food; it is the heart of the family home, the centre of activity and meeting, and in the middle is a large table at which the family eats. Next to it is the sitting-room, a quieter room for relaxation. It is equipped with sophisticated electronics – a television, recorders, electronic games and a synthesizer for making music – as well as a large shelf of books. The technological revolution has greatly reduced the cost of electronic machines of all kinds, and increased their durability and efficiency, so that almost every family can readily afford to own and run them. Beyond the sitting-room are the bedrooms and the bathroom, with a corridor running along the north side of the house. The house is one storey, with a single gable, to make the construction simpler and to enable every room to open directly on to the garden. A few yards from the house is a workshop and garage where the family can make simple articles of furniture and equipment, repair those that are damaged or faulty, store garden tools and keep and maintain the car.

Half the land belonging to each family is devoted to the intensive cultivation of vegetables. The vegetable area contains a number of small movable transparent tunnels which are placed above the seedlings in the early stages of growth. In addition there is a conservatory for the cultivation of seedlings in winter and spring, and for plants such as tomatoes, aubergines and cucumbers which grow to maturity through the summer and autumn. Thus, after a few seasons of intermittent gluts and shortages, the newcomer can learn to provide vegetables throughout the year, by calculating the maturity of the perishable vegetables such as lettuce to give a steady flow, and by storing the more durable vegetables like potatoes and carrots in a shed adjoining the workshop. Apart from a lawn for children to play and adults to relax on, most of the rest of the land is a small orchard; and under the trees geese and chickens graze, needing only the waste food from the house plus a small amount of additional grain to add to their diet of grass, natural seeds and worms. Between the orchard and the vegetable garden are rows of soft fruit bushes: gooseberries, redcurrants, blackcurrants and raspberries. Some families also grow a small area of lucerne, which is then crushed to give an almost tasteless juice; this is added to food to provide almost all the protein a person needs.

Most families own a small freezer for short-term storage of food; in addition, a few families own very large freezers – the size of a room – which are more economical to run; and they hire out space to nearby families for longer-term food storage. Manure to fertilize the land is bought partly from the nearby dairy farms and partly from the village sewerage works, where the waste is digested using heat obtained from its own methane, producing a residue of rich fertilizer. Thus, with land under cultivation of less than a quarter of an acre, and with a diet less dependent on meat than that of their parents and grandparents, a family can provide over half of the food it needs.

The active village

Just as the productive activities within the home have greatly expanded, providing directly for the family's needs, so too have the number of family-based businesses producing goods and services for sale both within the village and beyond.

There are almost thirty small workshops in Wickwyn, some run by a single person but most with two or more people working in partnership. They produce consumer goods where imaginative design catering for diverse needs and tastes gives the small business an advantage over the large corporation. Thus there are people making furniture, clothes, toys, household fittings such as lampstands and picture frames, and a small printer and publisher. The range of crafts is greater even than that of Wickwyn in its medieval heyday, but the methods of production are very different. The typical workshop contains highly-sophisticated machinery – purchased from large companies – which uses micro-electronic controls and laser beams for fashioning materials; and although a few traditional materials such as wood are still used, so also are many synthetic materials whose properties precisely suit the needs of the product. Thus the art of the craftsman lies less in his manual ability, and more in the ingenuity of design and in the choice and programming of machines.

The total area of the parish of Wickwyn is just under 1,800 acres, which by the late twentieth century was divided into two large farms. Now, as land prices have fallen and the large capital-intensive farm is no longer financially viable, land has been sold to newcomers in small plots, some as little as ten or twenty acres. There cereals and pulses are grown, and herds of cattle and sheep are kept. The individual farmer can afford to own only the smaller tools and machines, and so a Wickwyn Farmers' Co-operative has been formed, of which the farmers themselves are shareholders. It hires out machinery, such as tractors and harvesters; it has various machines for milling and processing what is grown, including one for drying grass, using solar power to turn it into winter feedstuff; and it organizes the packaging and marketing of produce within the village and at the market in Peterthorpe. Compared with the twentieth century the methods of cultivation are more labour-intensive, requiring smaller machines and fewer chemicals, and the mixture of arable farming and livestock means that straw and slurry can fertilize the soil. Thus the landscape has returned to how it was in the nineteenth century. The large fields have been divided up and the hedgerows restored, to reflect the smaller size of holdings and the demise of the huge machine. The different uses of the fields, for various crops and for grass, means that they form a patchwork of different colours, varying through the seasons.

About a mile south of the village, at the bottom of a hill, is a brickworks. It is on the same site as the brickworks that flourished briefly in the nineteenth century, and produces a cream and pink brick using the heavy clay which forms the subsoil of the area. Almost all the new buildings are constructed with this local brick, since the cost of lorry transport has risen greatly, making imported heavy materials more expensive. So, as in former times, the appearance of the buildings in Wickwyn, in common with villages elsewhere, reflects the geology of the local environment.

To the west of the village the ground slopes upwards, and the parish boundary is on the top of a ridge. On this ridge there are the remains of the old windmill where the peasant farmers used to bring their grain to be milled. Now a number of people have bought small areas of land for windfarms, and forty modern windmills, using propellors rather than sails, produce on average all the electricity for the village. The electricity is fed directly into the national grid, and it is metered so that the owners of the windmills are paid for what they produce. Today, total consumption of electricity is much lower than it was in the late twentieth century, partly due to the improved natural heating and insulation of houses, but also due to the greater efficiency of electric machinery and lighting, and to the decline of large-scale, energy-intensive industry. Thus most of the nation's electric energy is generated by small-scale local businesses, using mainly natural means such as wind power, as in Wickwyn, or water power in the more hilly parts of the country; only a small proportion is generated by large power stations using fossil fuels. So, instead of the pollution and the ugliness of the power stations, and the huge pylons marching across the countryside, the visible signs of electricity production are horizons, such as that to the west of Wickwyn, forested with tall elegant windmills whirring in the breeze.

Despite the far greater degree of local production, there are many products which the people of Wickwyn must continue to buy from outside. Four of the shops near the village green sell the food and basic provisions that cannot be produced in the village, from tea and sugar to matches and light bulbs. There is a butcher and an abbatoir, stocking meat imported into the village, and slaughtering and butchering locally-reared animals. Another shop sells stationery, newspapers, confectionery and a small range of books and tapes. For other goods, such as domestic appliances, as well as the specialized items made by small businesses in other villages, people travel to the shops in Peterthorpe. On the outskirts of the village there are three builders' merchants, which sell all the light materials needed for building construction and maintenance, and two plant-hire businesses which hire out tools and machinery.

Most families own a car or van, and private transport continues to be the main means of travel. But average mileage is low, and the vehicles are light and efficiently designed, so that fuel consumption is small. The majority of journeys are to Peterthorpe, to buy and sell goods, to visit the theatre and other entertainments in the city, and in some cases for work. For holidays most people travel as widely across the country and beyond as they did in the twentieth century, since living in such a diverse and pluriform village as Wickwyn increases rather than reduces people's interest and curiosity about how others live. Thus, although there is far less commuting than in the twentieth century, and so total travel is much reduced, the breadth of travel is as great as before. Some of the older and younger people, however, do not own vehicles and depend on public transport. To meet this need two small businesses have started in Wickwyn, operating a minibus service from a bus shelter on the village green; running mainly to Peterthorpe and back, but also going occasionally to other towns further afield, and arranging holiday trips. From Peterthorpe there are coach companies operating services to major cities and towns throughout the country.

Marriage and friendship

In the medieval village people were under great pressure to conform to a single pattern of behaviour. Not only did the

Church – and by implication God himself – seem to demand social conformity; but, as in any small community, people themselves made failure to conform extremely unpleasant by the simple, yet powerful, tool of gossip. Any unusual behaviour would become the subject of intense curiosity and of sanctimonious interest, so that people would seek to avoid such attention by conforming, or at least by misbehaving with discretion. By the end of the industrial age in the late twentieth century society had moved to the opposite extreme, when there was no moral rule that was not open to question, and where there was a baffling variety of different patterns of behaviour.

In the modern village there is both the moral and the social stability which medieval society enjoyed, but at the same time the tolerance and the flexibility of industrial society. The stability is due partly to the simple fact that people move house less frequently, and so there is time for deep roots to grow. But more fundamentally, it is because people's emotional needs are more fully satisfied in a community in which husband and wife have far greater common daily interest, and yet are also part of a network of friends and companions. For some newcomers, whose marriages are already weak, the greater sharing of material tasks and of daily decisions proves intolerable, revealing that the relationship cannot be sustained, and so they separate. But for most the challenge of working together for a common purpose renews and strengthens their marriage. Yet, as in the medieval village, daily life brings families constantly into touch with other families: helping one another at harvest time or in the building and maintaining of their homes, buying and selling goods; at meetings within the village; and simply chatting in the village lanes and pubs. Husband and wife are no longer so dependent on one another for emotional fulfilment since they have close friends beyond the home – and so are better able to be good friends to one another. Thus marriages are no longer so prone to snap under the weight of unrealistic expectations, and divorce has become comparatively rare simply because it is less necessary.

The pattern of family life, however, varies widely. In medieval society there was a strict division of tasks between men and women, regardless of the particular gifts individuals might have. The women spun and wove cloth, cooked meals and nurtured children, while their menfolk ploughed and sowed the fields, maintained the cottage, and chopped wood for the fire. In industrial society, in the name of equality between the sexes, women increasingly aspired to male roles, seeking employment in jobs that men did. The successful women who thus tried to combine a career with motherhood often had to employ a younger unmarried girl to take over much of the care of home and children. In the modern village there is no strict division of roles, and nor is there a difference in status given to work done within the family and work for which money is received. Couples divide the tasks between them not according to sex, but according to natural ability and inclination. The rearing of children is largely shared in families where husband and wife are in and around the house for much of the day, although if one parent has a greater gift in the care of children he or she gives more time to this. There are almost as many women as men working in the local businesses and farms, and often husband and wife work together, specializing in different aspects of a business.

The changes in family life have also brought a change in people's sexual attitudes. The greater stability and emotional satisfaction of married life means that there is no longer an obsession with physical sex, and the crude eroticism and open promiscuity of the twentieth century are now regarded with distaste. Yet neither is there the prudery of an earlier age, in which the sexual act was regarded as sinful. There is a greater realism about sex; that for some couples at some periods of their marriage physical sex may be a source of great pleasure and joy, but that emotional fulfilment in marriage can outweigh sexual disappointment; that adultery damages the trust on which marriage depends, but that this trust can be renewed after an adulterous relationship. There is also greater tolerance towards homosexuals, which in turn has led to the expectation that, rather than being moral outcasts free of any constraint on their promiscuity, they too should live as faithful couples. The old assertion that homosexuality is a physical perversion is not so much refuted as regarded as irrelevant, since the emotional love between people of the same sex can be as deep and as lasting as that between heterosexuals. So, although there remains some disapproval, homosexual couples can live openly together as part of the village community without being ridiculed or ostracized.

Despite – or rather because of – its impossibility, the moral ideal to which people aspired in industrial society was the perfect marriage partnership; indeed, the term 'moral' was taken to apply almost wholly to marital and sexual matters. In the modern village community it is the qualities of close friendship which are given the highest moral value. Within marriage itself, where husband and wife not only live but work together, it is mutual companionship that counts for far more than sexual love. And in the village as a whole people can clearly understand that the well-being and prosperity of the community depends on people's patience and gentleness, their concern and consideration for their neighbours. It is a symptom of this change in moral attitudes that the celibacy of Jesus Christ, so long an enigma to the Churches, now represents a moral ideal of which people can make sense: by choosing to be celibate he was able to offer himself in friendship freely and widely all around him. Though few follow the same path, those that do are respected for it.

4 Welfare

The rise and fall of the welfare state

In the medieval village children and old people participated in the economic life of the community: helping with the sowing and harvesting of crops, making and repairing tools and utensils, and maintaining the home. It was often grandparents who cared for the infants during the day, while the parents worked in the fields. Older children received most of their education by working with their parents, learning from them by example and practice. Those who were sick were nursed at home, with relatives and neighbours sharing the burden.

At first, in the new industrial cities of the nineteenth century, the welfare of the young, the sick and the old was largely ignored. As soon as they were able, children were compelled to work in factories and down mines by sheer economic necessity. While throwing raw sewage into ditches was dangerous enough in the medieval village, in the cities, where tens of thousands of people were packed together, it was disastrous, and disease was rampant. The unemployed, the disabled and those who survived to old age, sought to live by occasional earnings from casual work, or by the meagre poor relief provided by local authorities. The early decades of the nineteenth century saw a rapid increase in those claiming poor relief, and the rise in the cost of provision stimulated many respectable people, including the Archbishop of Canterbury, to advocate its abolition: it was claimed that poor relief simply stimulated the poor to have more children, and encouraged laziness, and so worsened their poverty. In 1834 a national system of workhouses was formed, replacing the old system of poor relief, whereby people could only receive support if they actually abandoned their homes and came to live in a large institution where the standard of life was deliberately kept below that of working people outside.

Yet, as the cities expanded, and as the middle and upper classes became more aware of the conditions of the urban population, so there was a growing concern for their well-being. Riots in the cities led to the fear of revolution since, as was rightly seen, discontented industrial workers could far more easily be organized for political agitation than the rural poor. But many, particularly the Christian evangelicals, felt not only fear but moral outrage at the suffering of their fellow human beings. The cause which attracted more widespread support was the education of children. While poor relief might only worsen poverty, education would have the opposite effect, enabling young people to work more productively and earn higher wages, so as to improve their position; and in doing so they would also stimulate economic progress in the nation as a whole. Expenditure on education could thus be seen as an investment – like the purchase of a new machine – bringing greater financial returns in the future. It was believed, moreover, that educated people would be far less inclined to riot and revolt, since they would see that their interests were best served by hard work for their employers.

The middle decades of the nineteenth century thus saw an enormous increase in voluntary schools, so that by the time elementary education became compulsory in 1870 nine out of ten children were already receiving it. They were funded partly by the Churches and other charitable bodies, and partly by subsidies paid by the State, but largely by the fees paid by the parents themselves. Their main tasks were to instill the basic skills of literacy and numeracy, and an acceptance of firm discipline. From the late nineteenth century onwards, the State took direct control of the majority of the schools, and expenditure on education multiplied, particularly in the mid-twentieth century after the Second World War, so that all children received free secondary as well as elementary education, and increasing numbers also received subsidized further education at college and university. This led to a subtle evolution in the purpose of education. The old desire for social control to prevent revolution was replaced by a new form of social engineering, the aim of which was to eliminate class distinction in society, so that in effect all would adopt the values and attitudes of the middle classes. The old discipline enforced by threat of punishment was abandoned in favour of a rigid system of examinations, in which almost every child participated, where the incentive of achieving academic success became the main external means of compelling hard work and orderly behaviour.

Alongside education, people also came to believe that the State should provide free health care. The early advocates in the nineteenth century used similar arguments to those justifying subsidized education: that a healthy work-force would be more productive, and would be more contented and so less liable to revolution. From the mid-nineteenth century onwards the State took direct charge of public health, ensuring proper sewage and the disposal of refuse. But it was not until the late twentieth century that the State took over the health care of individuals. The founders of the National Health Service believed that it was within the State's capacity to provide free health treatment on demand. Yet from the outset people's demands grew far more rapidly than the supply of doctors and hospitals, so queues became longer and costs multiplied. This was partly due to the greater sophistication of medical technology, but it was mainly a symptom of an attitude to health and sickness that by the late twentieth century had become firmly rooted in people's minds. Just as parents now handed over responsibility for the education of children to teachers, so people believed that they had little or no responsibility for their own health care, trusting unquestioningly the treatment given by doctors. The fact that both education and health care were provided free by the State, and were controlled by large government bureaucracies, only enhanced this attitude of passivity. The body was thus regarded as a machine to be maintained and repaired by experts, and individuals demanded from the doctors not advice on how to help themselves, but rather drugs and other treatment which could be received without explanation or understanding.

The advent of the factory in which people worked a specified number of hours for a set wage created a strict separation of work from retirement, and the reduction of the importance of the family home as a place of useful activity meant that old people had little domestic work to do. So the elderly ceased to be an asset to society, and instead became a burden to be supported. As the extended family network broke down, many old people could no longer live with their offspring, causing their poverty and isolation to become more acute. At the same time, in a society where religious faith was in decline death itself

44

came to be regarded as a failure to be dreaded, so that old people found themselves with neither purpose in life nor hope in death. At the beginning of the twentieth century the State began to pay pensions to the elderly, financed by contributions from those in employment. And as State health care became available and medical technology became more skilled at prolonging life, so the years of retirement lengthened.

The heyday of the Welfare State was in the period following the Second World War. The economist Keynes had taught that the government could maintain full employment by a high level of public expenditure, so that State welfare was justified not only for the direct benefit it provided, but also as an indirect means of boosting the economy. So for three decades the range of services widened and the costs grew, in the optimistic belief that the needs of the young, the sick and the old could be met by State action. But in the final years of the twentieth century the symptoms of failure became more acute. Discipline in secondary schools broke down, as teenagers with little prospect of examination success or paid employment saw no point in conforming to the demands of formal education. In health care there was growing doubt as to the value of the mechanical approach to people's well-being: psychological and psychosomatic diseases were more common, and conditions caused by bad diet and environment began to increase, despite the comparative affluence which people enjoyed.

Above all, the sheer cost of the Welfare State became intolerable. Rising unemployment had caused expenditure on social security payments to increase to just under one-fifth of the national income by the mid-1980s; and total welfare expenditure was almost one third of national income. This continued to increase sharply, due to unemployment continuing to worsen and then, after the turn of the century, due to the numbers reaching retirement age rising sharply – the result of the high birth-rates in the late 1940s and early 1960s. Yet the very forces that were causing the problems to increase meant that the number of people able to pay these costs through taxation – those in paid employment – was dropping sharply. So great had people's dependence become on welfare provision that severe cuts proved politically disastrous for government ministers who sought to impose them. Defenders of the Welfare State cried for cuts instead to defence expenditure, but total defence spending in the mid-1980s was less than 20% of welfare spending; and the proportion of income already paid in various forms of taxation was already one half of total national income.

So in the latter years of the twentieth century public attitudes to the Welfare State were caught in a contradiction. On the one hand, the poor were losing faith in the value of State education and health care; it was clearly seen that burgeoning social security expenditure was a sign of economic failure; and people could not afford the ever-increasing rate of taxation to pay for the Welfare State. On the other hand, the prospect of being denied State welfare was horrific, for without it the underlying social and economic crisis would become intolerable. The Welfare State had thus become a bandage which itself made the wound worse. In practice, governments had no choice but gradually and painfully to unwind the bandage. The cure for the wound itself lay outside the power of government, and was found through the actions of ordinary people in their own new communities.

Neighbourhood education

At first, new families in Wickwyn had to send their children each day by bus or car to State-run schools in Peterthorpe, the old village school having long since been closed. But, apart from the inconvenience of travel, the school itself was poorly equipped and, more importantly, it was understaffed, as the government funds for education had become so scarce. A few parents opted to teach their children at home.

As the number of children in the village grew, a group of enterprising parents came together to form a charitable trust to start a new village school. The building itself, on a site next to the village green, was constructed by the parents themselves, who also raised money for the cost of materials. The school is a single-storey terrace of classrooms, workshops and laboratories, all facing southwards to minimize the cost of heating, with a corridor at the rear. In the centre is the school hall, standing higher than the rest with a small clock-turret at the top, so that the overall shape is that of many old Victorian schools. The village green serves as the playground for the children, and in one corner near the school play equipment such as swings and slides has been installed. The school now educates most of the villagers' children. It has only a small number of paid trained staff, whose main task is to design and supervise the overall teaching programme; much of the actual work with the children themselves, as well as the maintenance and administration of the school, is done by parents and other volunteers. Some of the parents simply pay to send their children to the school, and the money is used to pay the staff and to purchase materials and equipment. But parents working for the school can send their children at little or no cost, depending on the amount of work done; and other volunteers, many of whom are grandparents, can nominate a child to benefit in this way. The responsibility for the well-being of the school lies with the trustees, who are elected by the parents; and they not only appoint the paid staff but also decide who can work voluntarily.

The education the children receive reflects a fresh understanding of the nature of education. Education in the nineteenth and twentieth centuries took children out of their normal situation and put them into the artificial environment of a classroom. There they were taught ideas, information and skills which, as far as the child could see, had little application to ordinary life. These had to be learnt because the teacher said they were important, and this reflected the wider demands of the world of work, which was quite foreign to the child's experience. Though many children flourished in the classroom, many others became permanently resistant to education.

In the modern village the child can be far more involved with the economic and social life of the family; thus education is both at home and at school, each complementing the other. At home children learn skills from their parents which are visibly useful, and at school the knowledge and skills they acquire – including mathematics, science and technical subjects, as well as reading and writing – can often find ready applications in daily life. The more purely academic subjects with no immediate practical application, such as history, geography and literature, can be taught mainly in the form of stories which capture the child's imagination; it is not until adulthood that people more naturally want to pursue knowledge of the arts for their own sake. The outward order and discipline of the school is strict compared with schools of the late twentieth century. But although there are punishments for misbehaviour – a not uncommon sight is recalcitrant children running round the village green at break-time – the main means of discipline is the sense of purpose which the children themselves now feel; children are naturally eager to acquire the skills and knowledge which enable them to emulate adults. Only when they turn to the arts is there relative disorder, when the teacher may ask them to enact a drama, play music, or paint pictures to illustrate a story.

Formal schooling ends at the age of sixteen, when the young person is given an aptitude assessment, rather than having to sit formal examinations. The assessment's purpose is not to grade young people in a single order of ability, as the old exams sought to do, but rather to advise them as to their possible vocations. The assessments are organized by the government, in consultation with the local teachers, and the aptitude report is given to the young person to use when applying for work and higher education. The majority of young people start work as apprentices in the various small businesses within the village, in the factory in Wickwyn itself, or in a firm in Peterthorpe. In the latter half of the twentieth century most firms had given up taking apprentices, because the frequent changing of jobs meant that few of their apprentices stayed with them after training and thus the firm received little benefit from the cost it had incurred. Today, firms want to take apprentices because the greater stability of life means that people seldom move from their original firm, and so the firm enjoys the benefit of the training it gives. Many of the apprentices also go on courses for short periods at the university in Peterthorpe, supported by their firms. A few young people, with a capacity for pure academic work, continue in full-time higher education at university; and if their aptitude assessment supports this path, they are funded by government scholarships.

Higher education itself has evolved to reflect the changing nature of society, and has recovered much of the flexibility that universities enjoyed before the industrial age. Thus courses of study are now tailored to suit the particular needs of individuals. Universities are smaller, and almost every major town such as Peterthorpe has its own university, embracing all aspects of higher education. Each student, whether full-time or part-time, is given a director of studies whose job it is to help the student to decide his pattern of study. As in the traditional Scottish universities, the university provides lecture halls and authorizes lecturers to put on courses, while students pay a fee to attend – which provides the lecturer's income. Just as this system in the seventeenth and eighteenth centuries gave Scotland the reputation for having the brightest lectures in Europe, so the quality of lectures in the modern university is very high, and lecturers seek to attract students by responding directly to their needs. Lecturers are free to decide how many lectures they will give, and people from various walks of life are authorized to give occasional courses. In addition, in each field of study the students are allocated to tutors who supervise their reading, essay writing, and their work in the laboratories; here, too, the student pays fees to the supervisor, with the university providing the necessary facilities.

Most young students study the natural sciences and business subjects which have direct relevance to future work. The arts subjects, however, attract more older students. Many study part-time, while others, perhaps after their families have grown up, take a year or more away from their normal work to study full-time.

Local village schools, such as that at Wickwyn, also apply to the university for lecturers to come and give evening courses for adults, on a similar basis to those at the university itself: the local school provides the facilities, and the fees of those who attend pay the lecturer. Thus Wickwyn typically has a university course running at the school on most weekday nights, attended by between ten and twenty people. The universities continue to set examinations for which people may choose to enter, regardless of how much or how little formal tuition they have received. The exams are organized on a similar basis to those of the old Open University, founded in the twentieth century: students are awarded credits, which may be of value in themselves in applying for employment, and which may also be counted towards a degree. Apart from providing tuition, the universities remain places of academic research, funded by government, and many of those giving lectures also derive a steady income as permanent research fellows. This research, as in the past, provides the scientific basis for many of the technological innovations in industry.

In all, the total resources devoted to education, both in schools and universities, is greater than ever before. The burden on government, however, is much less, since much of the labour is given freely by those whose children stand to benefit, and financial costs are largely borne by parents and employers. And the fact that parents are directly involved in the running of schools, and parents, students and employers alike are contributing directly for the benefit that they receive, ensures a high quality of tuition.

Neighbourhood health care

Just as the first newcomers to Wickwyn had to send their children to Peterthorpe for education, so also they had to travel there for medical treatment. And just as the State schools had become demoralized and dilapidated, so the National Health Service was suffering the agony of trying to meet ever greater needs on ever smaller resources. The general hospital in Peterthorpe had become shabby, its paintwork and its floor coverings peeling, and its standards of hygiene falling. As Wickwyn grew, so a group of people formed a local charitable trust to build and run a clinic in the village, with a dispensary and a small hospital, in much the same way as the school was founded. It is a cluster of single-storey buildings lying southwest of the church, facing the village green; the buildings are spaciously laid out, with lawns and flower-beds around them.

There is a single doctor and a small number of nurses, living in the village, providing the specialized treatment; most of the initial diagnosis and treatment, formerly done exclusively by doctors, is now done by the nurses, who refer only more complex cases to the doctor. In addition, much of the daily care of the patients in the hospital, the cooking of meals, the maintenance of the buildings and the administration, is done by volunteers. As in the school, the trustees have overall responsibility, appointing both the paid staff and the volunteers, and they in turn are elected by the registered patients. The volunteers receive treatment without paying, according to the amount of work they do; other patients pay a fixed amount each year, entitling them to receive treatment as and when they need it – thus in effect providing an insurance against the uncertainty of when illness will occur. For major treatment, people still go to the central hospital in Peterthorpe, which has been revitalized. It is still run by the government, but is now adequately funded, partly by the contributions of local trusts such as that at Wickwyn, who pay for their patients to use it, and partly by individuals not belonging to such trusts who pay a National Health Tax.

The formation of local trusts has been part of a transformation in people's attitudes to health care. The fact that the trusts are formed and run by the patients themselves reflects a new sense of personal responsibility that individuals have towards their own well-being. When illness occurs, the doctor or nurse discuss with the patient the most appropriate form of treatment, recognizing that healing depends on the right mental and emotional attitudes, as well as on physical means. And, since they are themselves part of the community which they serve, the doctor and the nurses can come to know their patients intimately, and can more easily understand the wider spiritual, mental and social conditions of the patients which may contribute to their illnesses. Thus, just as education no longer plucks the child out of his normal environment, but can embrace the whole life of the child, so too the modern health service, by working in partnership with its patients, can care for the whole life of the patient.

This greater sense of personal responsibility encourages people to learn more about the workings of the body, and so to take greater care personally of their own health. For most simple ailments people are now far more willing and able to decide on their own treatment, without recourse to the clinic. More importantly, the movement which began in the late twentieth century towards more wholesome ways of daily living, has now become part of the common culture of the community. People continue to eat meat and sugar, but in far smaller quantities; some families only having meat dishes and puddings once a week or on special occasions. Consumption of fresh vegetables, fruit, and foods made from wholemeal grains, has risen. Many families make their own wines and beers, and the two local pubs are – as pubs have always been – more popular places for social gathering than the church; but there is little regular heavy drinking. And the fact that even those with quite sedentary paid occupations have far more time to work at home on their land and in their workshops means that people are physically much fitter, without need of gymnasia and squash courts. In the school, health education is an important part of the curriculum; and so from childhood people accept without question the basic rules of healthy living – just as many children a few generations ago subsisted largely on sweets, sodas and fried food, without they or their parents questioning the dire consequences of such a diet, because they were not taught otherwise.

The new pattern of life has led to greater mental stability, and has made the social consequences of mental illness far less damaging. Acute depression and anxiety, which had reached epidemic proportions in the late twentieth century, is now less common as people feel more secure and less isolated. Those prone to depression and despair no longer find the external world so threatening, and so the compulsion to withdraw into inner blackness is less strong. And those prone to anxiety and nervous exhaustion find life less bewildering and uncertain in its demands, and so less stressful. Suicide and attempted suicide are now comparatively rare, as social bonds have strengthened, and so individuals are less liable to regard themselves as without value or purpose to others. There remain a few people whose mental illness is so acute that they live permanently or intermittently in a small house within the village hospital. Yet even they need not be cut off from the wider community since, as with the village idiots of medieval times, their erratic behaviour soon becomes familiar to people, and so they are welcomed in the local shops, the pubs and the church.

Ageing and dying

The new arrivals to Wickwyn are mostly young or in early middle age, and for the first twenty or thirty years of its expansion the village was dominated by young families. But within one or two generations, as the first newcomers grew into old age, the proportions of differing age groups became more natural.

Yet in the daily life of the village, the distinction between young and old, employed and retired, is far less than in the industrial city. And the elderly, rather than being regarded – and regarding themselves – as burdens on society past any useful contribution, are now valued for the qualities that old age can bring. The path through life for many follows the four stages of life taught by the Hindu sages, which was implicit also in the medieval view of man's life cycle. The first two stages are ones of intense activity: the child learning the skills and knowledge necessary for the productive life, and the 'householder' working hard to look after the family and to fulfil personal ambitions. In the third stage of life, after the family has grown up, the person can work less intensively, and be more patient and reflective in what he does. And in the final stage, when the person is capable of little or no productive work, a good and well-spent life will bear fruit in wisdom and insight which, if sought and appreciated by younger people, is the most valuable contribution of all.

Thus many people in late middle age, when their children are old enough to support themselves, give up paid employment or running a business and devote themselves to unpaid work and to study, depending on savings for their limited financial needs. Much of the voluntary administration of the school and the clinic is done by people in this age group. As their children establish their own homes and start families, they often share in the care of their grandchildren, especially during the day when the parents are busy. And they may help, too, in much of the lighter work requiring greater patience, such as cultivating seedlings in greenhouses, and making and mending clothes. Many also attend university courses, either in the village school in the evening, or in some cases going to lectures and tutorials in Peterthorpe; a high proportion of those studying the arts subjects, such as literature and history, are people in their fifties, sixties and even seventies, who can dedicate far more time than younger students to the extensive reading that such courses require.

Only in the final years of life do people withdraw from such activity. Yet in most cases they are able to stay within their own

53

homes, continuing to look after their own needs as far as possible, and receiving additional domestic help from family and neighbours. To avoid the sense of being burdensome, some old people come to an agreement with one or more younger families, that the young people give such help as is needed in exchange for the use of the old person's land. Thus only very few, who require constant nursing, need live in the village hospital, which has a house for this purpose. Some old people, as has always been the case, grow bitter and resentful as the years pass and as physical faculties fail; but their continuing involvement in the community makes it easier for the elderly to resist this temptation, and instead to find those qualities of undemanding love and wise tolerance that are the special virtues of age.

In the Litany of the old Anglican service book, composed in the sixteenth century, there is a prayer that one should be spared from sudden death. Although people have always had a natural fear of death, in those days they wished to be prepared for it because their religious faith taught them of the 'communion of saints': that death is not the end of life, but rather the pathway to the perfect unity of all God's people. This echoed the more tribal understanding of the Hebrew people in the Old Testament, that in death the person is 'gathered to his fathers'. But the individualism of industrial society, in which corporate ties were weakened and broken, destroyed such an attitude to death. The Christian Churches taught a more individualistic doctrine of eternal life, that the person received a reward or compensation for actions and events on earth. Most people were unconvinced and could see death only as extinction, since it visibly destroyed their existence as individuals. Thus death became a subject that was distasteful and embarrassing to mention, and people in general wanted to die suddenly without warning. Only in times of war did a sense of corporate solidarity re-emerge, and people could face the imminent prospect of death with courage, and could speak honestly of being willing to die for their fellows.

The renewal of a sense of community in villages such as Wickwyn has enabled death once more to be spoken of with honesty, and for the very old openly to look forward to death without being regarded as morbid. People no longer want a sudden death, but rather a good death in which physical pain is minimized, and in which they can sense, amidst the fear and sorrow, that their purpose on earth has been fulfilled. This in turn has changed the way in which the dying are treated. Previously, people with terminal illnesses were frequently not told of their prospects, and a barrier of mutual pretence became established between the dying person and his or her loved ones. Often great efforts were made to prolong physical life by artificial means, even at the expense of greater suffering and distress. Now the dying are told of their prospects as a matter of course, to allow them to prepare for death; and the main purpose of those treating them is to enable them to die in as much physical and emotional comfort as possible, even when this means using pain-killing drugs that may shorten life, and not attempting to cure additional illnesses such as pneumonia. The old moral debate about euthanasia, which doctors frequently but illicitly practised, has ceased to apply, since the choice is no longer perceived as between prolonging life or hastening death. Rather, there is a common purpose that death should be a peaceful conclusion to physical life.

5 Politics

The myth of political ideologies

In the medieval village, the life of the individual was governed by the position in society in which he found himself. Property was vested in the lord of the manor to be used communally, and people were bound together in ties of mutual obligation, hallowed by generations of custom and tradition. The agricultural and industrial revolutions broke these ancient ties. Property became the possession of private individuals, and people were free to use their land, capital and labour as they chose, in pursuit of the highest profits and wages. There were no mutual obligations beyond honesty and fairness in financial transactions, and central authority was reduced to a minimum.

Behind this change lay a powerful ideology which had its philosophical roots in Isaac Newton's view of the universe. His studies of astronomy led him to believe that the natural universe worked with perfect order, the heavenly bodies moving in complete harmony with one another, set in motion by a benevolent God who then withdrew from all further involvement with his creation. This doctrine, which became known as Deism, gained widespread support, and inspired people to think that the social order should be similar to the natural order, that God has so designed humanity that individuals acting freely would live in harmony one with another. The political economist Adam Smith in the late eighteenth century wrote of the 'invisible hand' that causes the self-interest of individuals in pursuing the highest material gain for themselves to lead to the greatest good of all. The labourer should seek the highest wage and the owner of capital the maximum profit, since wages and profits reflect the productive value of labour and capital. And individuals should spend their income freely according to their own wants, since the force of consumer demand in a competitive market would cause firms to produce goods to satisfy those wants. This ideology came to be known as *laissez-faire*, since the government should not interfere in the free actions of individuals, but confine itself to the protection of private property through the provision of a police force and military defence.

The myth of the invisible hand gained a powerful grasp on popular imagination in the nineteenth century, and the burgeoning growth of industry operating freely in response to market forces seemed to confirm the truth of this new faith. Fables were written for children in which the spread of the free market across the country and the world was portrayed as the victory of good over evil, of truth over ignorance. The political economists who followed Smith were held in great esteem as the apostles of the invisible hand, and progressive families, when employing a governess for their children, would require not only a familiarity with the Bible but also knowledge of the rudiments of political economy. The Churches themselves saw *laissez-faire* and the Christian gospel as complementary, the one offering material well-being and the other spiritual grace; and many of the industrialists who devoted six days of the week to working at the altar of economic expansion would, on the seventh, be prominent among those kneeling at the altar of Christ.

Thus, within a century, tens of thousands of villages such as Wickwyn which had been largely self-sufficient, producing for themselves most of what they consumed, had become tiny threads in a vast, complex web of commerce. The grain they grew on the land was mostly sold to the cities, where it competed with grain imported from across the globe, so that the price they received depended on harvest throughout the world; a bumper harvest in Europe or America could depress the price per ton of Wickwyn grain, even when its own harvest was poor. In return for selling their grain, the people of Wickwyn bought manufactured goods from the cities and from abroad: cloth from Lancashire made from Indian cotton; tea from Ceylon and China, and sugar from the West Indies; iron tools from the furnaces in the north-east of England – an ever-expanding range of products superior in quality and cheaper in price than those traditionally produced in the village.

The triumph of the free market depended, however, on a widening gap between the rich and the poor. The income people received was in proportion to the value of the work and resources they contributed to production. So those who were successful accumulated more resources to become yet richer, while the others, unable to build up resources, remained poor. Thus, in the industrial cities of the nineteenth century, as the output of the factories expanded and their owners prospered, there was widespread poverty and disease among the ordinary workers. It was this gross inequality that opened the way for an alternative ideology, that of State socialism, which looked to the central government to provide help and to redress injustice. In its fullest form socialism required that the State owned all capital, so that everyone would be working in state enterprises and the profits from capital would go to the State. In the twentieth century many countries experienced socialist revolutions, in which the new leaders sought to apply this ideology. In Britain, as in most other Western countries that were spared revolutions, governments adopted a diluted socialism, trying to combine a free market in some sectors with State ownership in others. Major public utilities and basic industries, such as electricity supply and coal-mining, were nationalized; and in addition the State provided, through taxation, a wide range of free and subsidized services, from health care and education to refuse disposal and cheap housing.

Most saw socialism as opposed to the ideology of *laissez-faire*, and politics both within nations and across the world became divided between socialism and *laissez-faire* capitalism. The rhetoric of socialism proclaimed a brotherhood amongst working people, seeking to re-create the corporate solidarity of the medieval village, while still enjoying the fruits of industrial production. Yet in truth socialism was merely an amended form of capitalism. The scale of production under socialism remained large and impersonal, and there was still a free market in the buying of goods and the selling of labour; the only difference was that the State had replaced the stock exchange as the provider of financial capital. The welfare services provided by the State did not create a sense of brotherhood, but were a substitute for self-reliance and the mutual obligations that had been part of the close-knit medieval community.

In the mid-twentieth century, the involvement of government in economic and social life expanded rapidly. The economic depression and unemployment of the 1920s and 1930s, and the fact that massive spending on arms during the Second World War had cured the depression, convinced politicians that a high level of government spending on social welfare could maintain full employment and improve living standards. For two-and-a-half decades it seemed that a partnership between government and private enterprise offered the prospect of ever-increasing prosperity: that free world markets, combined with a high level of domestic public expenditure, would lead to uninterrupted economic growth, and would eventually abolish poverty throughout the world.

But within ten years, during the 1970s, this optimism turned to pessimism as inflation, followed by steeply-rising unemployment and economic stagnation, seemed to defy the efforts of government and private enterprise alike. Politics rapidly became polarized, and extreme solutions appealed to a bewildered and frustrated electorate. Right-wing politicians looked back to the original ideology of *laissez-faire*, renewing their faith in the invisible hand; the current problems, they pronounced, were due to the encroachment of the State on economic affairs, and prosperity and full employment could be restored by freeing individuals from State control. Left-wing politicians turned instead to the original values of socialism, stating that the failure was due to insufficient co-operation between people, and that only through greater collective action could a solution be found. For a period during the 1980s and early 1990s, the depth of the crisis in Britain was partly disguised by the discovery of oil in the North Sea: its revenues enabled governments to maintain the welfare services and to pay benefits to the increasing number of unemployed people without having to raise taxation. But by the turn of the century the impotence of both ideologies, *laissez-faire* and State socialism, could no longer be hidden: it became obvious that neither right-wing nor left-wing policies could restore the industrial economy of earlier decades.

Both ideologies, however, contained truths that proved vital to the new pattern of life that emerged. People needed freedom from State control in order to create for themselves ways of living that could satisfy both their material and their social needs. Only through such freedom, in which individuals became personally responsible for their social and material lives,

59

could society begin to rediscover a spirit of co-operation and a common purpose.

Local self-rule

The people migrating from the cities to the villages are not in most cases motivated by any political ideology. Relatively few consciously see themselves as participating in a social and economic revolution as important and far-reaching as the Industrial Revolution of two-and-a-half centuries ago. Most are simply responding to the force of circumstance, sensing that this new way of life may be more prosperous and fulfilling for themselves and their families. The life that has become established in Wickwyn and elsewhere combines the ideologies of capitalism and socialism, and transforms those ideologies by infusing them with the more personal moral values of medieval society. Individuals enjoy the freedom of *laissez-faire* capitalism: they own their houses; many own land, small businesses and company shares; and they can buy and sell goods and services as they wish. As under socialism, a high proportion of resources and time is given to social welfare – to education and health care. Yet in the modern village, in which through the daily business of life people come into close contact with their neighbours, and in which people came to depend on one another materially and emotionally, economic decisions are rooted in personal relationships, and self-interest is constantly tempered by a sense of mutual obligation.

The role of government is now largely confined to its three ancient tasks: the maintenance of law and order; the protection of the weak and vulnerable; and the provision of those services which individuals cannot provide for themselves. The old parish council of Wickwyn and similar villages, which had declined in importance as the village declined, is now a major body of local government. It provides sewerage and refuse disposal, it runs a small fire brigade, it maintains the local lanes and the village green. The county planning departments, which became so powerful in the twentieth century, are now much reduced in size and power, and work in co-operation with parish council planners: they cannot prevent new building, but they plan the layout of roads and main drainage, and so can advise individuals on where to build in order to have easy access to these services; their only power is to ensure the health and safety of new buildings. The parish council also employs a small group of part-time constables, whose task is to patrol the parish; they can make arrests, but must report all crime and hand over suspects to the county police force. As the parish council has grown in importance, and as local trusts have taken over much of the education and health services, so the county councils and central government have diminished. Their function now is to employ inspectors to visit local schools and hospitals to ensure adequate standards are maintained; to run some schools and health centres, especially in urban areas, as well as running the universities and central hospitals; to build and maintain the main roads; and they are responsible for drawing up and enforcing laws to protect the environment. They continue to run a National Insurance scheme to provide a basic pension for the elderly, and benefits for the sick and unemployed; people are free to opt out of all or part of this scheme so long as they can show that they have adequate private provision. And they give, without prior contributions, an income to the disabled and the handicapped.

Public expenditure is thus now a fraction of its level in the late twentieth century, and taxation is correspondingly less. The main form of taxation is a cross between the old income tax and the expenditure taxes levied on goods: people are taxed on what they have actually spent on consumption of goods and services. Thus, as in the past, they must declare their financial income; in addition, they must declare their cash assets at the beginning and end of the year, and account for their savings through the year and for expenditure on items apart from consumer goods, such as machinery for business purposes. From this the tax authorities can calculate consumer spending, and determine what is owed in taxation. The comparatively low tax rate means that there is less incentive to cheat; moreover, it is not easy to cheat by overestimating expenditure on machinery and savings, since positive evidence must be given of this expenditure. This form of tax both encourages economic growth, since a person can reduce his tax burden by greater investment in machinery and higher savings; and it encourages family life since domestic production, where goods and services are produced within the family for its own consumption, is not subject to taxation. It is also progressive, falling more heavily on the rich than the poor, since in general poorer families produce a higher proportion of their needs within the home. There is also a further tax for those who continue to use the State health service and schools; but people who make adequate provision through the charitable trusts are exempt from this tax, thus encouraging the growth of such trusts.

The changing role of government has also changed the role of politicians and their parties. In the nineteenth and twentieth centuries the political parties which held sway embodied the conflicting interests of different groups in society. Division and mutual opposition in politics came to be regarded as inevitable, even desirable, and mirrored the deep social and economic divisions of industrial society. In the early and mid-nineteenth century it was the Tories, representing the old landed aristocracy feeling threatened by industrial change, who stood in opposition to the Liberals, representing the new industrial middle classes. The Liberals advocated free trade and open markets, knowing that this would bring high profits to the new factories, and were impatient of the Tories' apparent nostalgia for the old village. By the early twentieth century the ground had shifted. The old Tories were almost extinct, and the opposition was between those who continued to put their faith in free markets and the new Socialists, representing the interests of the working classes. Thus the old division between the aristocracy and the middle classes had been replaced in political life by the division between capitalist and worker.

The ordinary voter, however, while often deeply involved in the issues of the day, remained profoundly cynical of the political process and of the politicians who wielded power. Whereas the monarchs and the lords of old, however corrupt and unpopular they may sometimes have been, were still treated with deference – and even were believed to have been ordained by God to their positions of power – the party politicians were for the most part regarded with disrespect and suspicion. Politicians tried to elevate their activities by appealing to social ideals and moral visions, pretending that their opposition to other parties was ideological and ethical. But these ideologies had little attraction for the majority of people, and there remained a yearning for leaders whose honesty could be trusted, and who could somehow unify society with a sense of common purpose. Yet the nature of society itself made such unity impossible, and gave people little choice but to vote for the party which best expressed their own class interest.

The style of politics which has emerged in the twenty-first century, in response to the profound change in the whole social and economic order, answers this popular yearning. The opposing ideologies have simply ceased to be relevant, as people and local communities have become more self-reliant and so have stopped looking to politicians to further their interests. Since the government is no longer a major provider of people's needs, it cannot promote the claims of one group or class against another. Instead, in its more limited tasks of maintaining order and of protecting the vulnerable, people today, as they did in ancient time, regard the government as the guardian of justice in society. This in turn has bred a new type of politician. Formerly, politicians were required to be fighters for their own class or area, and their success was measured by their ability to further their sectional interests against the interests of others. To do this the politician had to belong to a strong and disciplined party. Now the old parties have evolved into groups where people debate the issues of the day, and at Wickwyn there are three such groups. Though each has its own tradition and bias, their views are not determined by opposing ideologies but are the outcome of free discussion; and frequently the parties find themselves in agreement. At election time each party puts up a candidate, and it is their perception of the candidate's honesty and wisdom, rather than party allegiance, which determines how people vote. A capacity to listen and respond to the needs of ordinary people, and to encourage a consensus within the community, rather than ideology and fighting ability, are the qualities that attract votes – and so are the qualities to which ambitious politicians must aspire.

Local industry

Just as in the medieval village, the home and the small workshop are again places where many of the goods which people need are produced. However, unlike the medieval village, industrial production in factories managed by large companies is also important, producing basic materials, machines and equipment for both business and domestic use. The Industrial Revolution has not been reversed, but rather the nature of industry has evolved, and since the twentieth century modern technology has enabled a radical shift in the location of industry. Now, instead of being concentrated in large cities in certain regions of the country and the world, it is spread, so that relatively small industrial plants and research centres are to be found in most large villages and towns.

The factory situated to the west of Wickwyn produces moulded synthetic materials for the interior bodywork of vehicles. The large transnational company to which it belongs makes a wide range of cars and vans, with designs adapted to the needs of each local market. The technological revolution has made both design and manufacture highly flexible, so that at relatively little cost basic designs can be adapted by computer, and the micro-electronic controls adjusted to produce comparatively small numbers of a particular model. This capacity to respond to local market conditions means that transnational companies need to have plants in every region where they sell their products. At the same time a high degree of automation has greatly reduced the number of people required in each plant, and for the most part the workers need to be highly skilled. Thus companies now typically situate their plants in villages such as Wickwyn, where the workers themselves wish to live, or in towns such as Peterthorpe within easy reach of village communities. The workers themselves generally work fairly short hours, prefer-ring a smaller salary in order to have more time at home. There is even greater flexibility when the work consists of processing and disseminating information, such as financial management, research and marketing. People can do much of their work at home, using computers linked by cable to their headquarters, and conducting many business meetings by telephone and closed-circuit television. Thus the companies with main offices in Peterthorpe have employees in Wickwyn and other sur-rounding villages who need to come into town at most only once or twice a week.

As the nature of economic life has changed, so too the finan-cial system has adapted. The banks during the nineteenth and twentieth centuries lent mainly to large firms, and usually rates of interest were low. But in the late twentieth century two

64

converging forces brought the banking system to the point of collapse. First, bank lending to countries in Asia and Latin America expanded rapidly in the 1970s as banks sought to reinvest the vast financial surpluses of the oil-producing nations. Second, as Western governments found that their tax revenues fell while expenditure on welfare benefits rose, they had to borrow increasing amounts of money from the public, driving up interest rates. As a result, many debtor countries and many companies were unable to service their loans, and defaulted. The financial crisis continued with intermittent bankruptcies until local communities became more economically self-reliant. Government financial requirements consequently diminished, and thus interest rates fell. The banks and other financial institutions which have survived, and the new banks which have been founded, while continuing to lend to big firms, now make a large proportion of their loans to individuals and small groups to buy property, to start businesses, and to finance the charitable trusts for education and health care. The banks no longer need numerous local branches handling cheques and cash, because almost all money transactions are by direct debit: when a purchase is made the customer's debit card is placed in a machine cabled to the banking system. However, banks employ local representatives, of which Wickwyn has seven, who arrange loans and manage people's savings; since they have personal knowledge of the individuals and small businesses with whom they deal, they are well-placed to make prudent decisions.

Peace and freedom

In 1982 a nuclear missile base was established three miles from Wickwyn, on an old wartime aerodrome at Brinsworth. At night-time, looking across the valley to the south of the village, one could see on the horizon a line of floodlights marking the perimeter fence. The new generation of weapons installed there was the latest phase in an arms race that dated back not merely forty years to the invention of the nuclear bomb, but to the previous century. In pre-industrial times warfare had involved hand-to-hand combat between soldiers; and although the quality of their weapons was important, the courage and morale

65

of the soldiers themselves was decisive. But from the late nineteenth century onwards, battles were increasingly fought on the
design boards and the production lines of the munitions factories, until by the end of the Second World War, with the
blanket bombing of cities, warfare involved whole populations
at the mercy of the lethal inventions of scientists. Industrialization had given humankind the power to destroy itself on a scale
far beyond the horrors of the most deadly medieval plague.

The arms race was the symptom of a paradox which lay at the
heart of industrialization itself and the ideals which it embodied.
As the new industries expanded in the nineteenth century, they
required ever wider markets for their products; and so Britain
led the way in breaking down the barriers of commerce and
establishing free trade across the world. The advocates of free
trade, like the great campaigners Cobden and Bright who toured
the country holding evangelistic rallies in its support, believed
that it would at last bring peace between the nations of the
world: once nations became dependent on one another for the
material necessities of life, they proclaimed, then war between
them would become inconceivable. Missionaries like Livingstone
believed that only when trading links had been made with the
tribes of Africa, through which they would realize the benefits
of European industrial goods, would the Churches then per-
suade them of the benefits of Christian civilization.

Yet, far from establishing peace, the spread of commerce
created the conditions for conflict. The peoples of Asia and
Africa, with whom the industrial nations traded, found their
own traditional economies overwhelmed by cheap manufactured goods, and they themselves were turned into primary
producers of raw materials for Western industry. This economic
subordination led in turn to political colonization, and the industrial nations sought to protect their commercial interests
from one another. Thus there was both growing rivalry between
the rich nations, which fostered the jingoism that led them so
enthusiastically into the First World War, and seeds of bitter
resentment were sown in the poorer nations towards their over-
lords, which grew into the bloody wars in which Asia and Africa
became entangled in the mid-twentieth century. Even after the
colonial empires were formally disbanded, the rivalry continued
to grow sharper, with the nations now divided into two ideological power blocs, capitalist and communist; they manoeuvred

and jostled to extend their spheres of influence, often causing the most terrible civil wars in the countries they sought to control. The habit of military rivalry and mutual distrust between the great powers became so deeply rooted that by the late twentieth century the original commercial stimulus had been forgotten, and political and military influence had become an end in itself.

The arrival of the nuclear base at Brinsworth brought the terror of this global conflict to the doorsteps of the affluent farmers and commuters of this quiet corner of the English countryside. Within weeks of the government's announcement of the advent of the missiles, a group of protesters had established a camp outside the main gates of the base, and an Anglican bishop came to celebrate Holy Communion to mark the camp's opening, in the belief that nuclear missiles were an affront to Christ's gospel of peace. Local people were outraged. The protesters were villified as layabouts, and the bishop was branded by many as a communist traitor. As the protest grew, and as Brinsworth became the scene of massive demonstrations against nuclear weapons, so the outrage turned to hysteria, and people refused even to leave their homes for fear that these would be looted by the protesters. The few local people who supported the anti-nuclear protest, and the protesters themselves, found themselves ostracized in the neighbourhood, ignored in the street and refused service in local pubs. They for their part frequently spoke of those who did not support their cause as warmongers, guilty of condemning the world to nuclear devastation. It was as if the same distrust which divided the power blocs themselves now divided the locality of Brinsworth: people of different ideologies were unable to live together in harmony and mutual respect.

Then as the months and years passed there was a gradual change of attitude among the people near Brinsworth. The demonstrators did not cause the damage to property that people feared, and were no more intolerable than the army convoys that rumbled through the villages to and from the base. But, more fundamentally, people came to see the personal conflicts not only as fruitless, but as based on failure of understanding. In truth, both sides shared a desire for peace and a horror of war, differing on whether disarmament by Britain would increase or reduce the prospect of preventing war; thus the division of view was not rooted in moral differences, but rather on a political assessment on which course was least dangerous. The first visible sign of a new attitude was on the day of the largest demonstration at Brinsworth. Outside the church at Wickwyn was a police road-block, beyond which the road was filled with the coaches and cars of demonstrators; while inside the church a quiet service was held to which people in the locality were invited to offer readings and prayers. While most local people stayed guarding their homes, a congregation of about forty, of different political views and even of different religious persuasions, assembled. In the tranquil atmosphere of the church, with the noise of the demonstration in the distance, right-wingers found themselves praying for the protesters and for the leaders of the communist bloc; while left-wingers prayed for the military and those who controlled the nuclear weapons.

The change of attitude around Brinsworth foreshadowed a similar change in public opinion as a whole. The focus of debate began to shift from the vexed question of military and political strategy to the underlying moral and emotional issues of the relations between nations. The actual existence of nuclear bombs – and of equally devastating weapons for germ warfare – came to be seen as secondary to the fact that the power blocs felt compelled to threaten one another at all. While Britain, even with her small arsenal of nuclear weapons, could in theory have devastated America, this possibility was never contemplated simply because there was sufficient trust between the two nations; it was the lack of trust between the power blocs that was the real threat to mankind. At the same time, people began to perceive a savage irony in the situation: that whereas it was the quest for economic and commercial dominance that originally stimulated the global rivalries during the colonial period, now this rivalry was threatening to cripple the economies of the powerful nations – the costs of the arms race continued to spiral, as ever more sophisticated weapons were invented; but as unemployment rose and tax revenues fell, so the capacity to pay these costs diminished. It became increasingly clear in the last years of the twentieth century, even among right-wing politicians, that the cost of the arms race was becoming insupportable; so, although thirty years of disarmament talks between the power blocs had brought almost no tangible results, economic pressure now gave the negotiations a new sense of urgency.

Then in the early decades of the twenty-first century the revolution in social and economic life began to alter fundamentally the relations between nations, and to eliminate the underlying causes of conflict. The renewal of local production, and the more even spread of industry across the world to serve local markets, brought a steep decline in the volume of international trade. Moreover, as local communities and nations became more self-reliant, the gross inequalities between different regions of the world which were such a marked feature of twentieth-century life were greatly reduced. Thus the incentive for one nation or group of nations to exert power and influence over others diminished. At the same time, communication between peoples increased: as trade in goods and raw materials fell, it was replaced by a greater flow of information and expertize across the world – since the research and development of the large transnational companies had global applications. This meant that in the course of their work many people employed by these companies travelled extensively, strengthening personal contacts and understanding between countries. Governments saw that it was in their national interest to encourage this flow, and so minimized the controls and restrictions on personal travel.

The combination of the sheer economic cost of weapons, added to the revolution in economic and social life, has meant that the great powers have now largely dismantled their vast arsenals of weapons. While military strategy has always been justified as defensive rather than aggressive, in the past this meant defending global interests and hence in practice involved aggression. Now, as such global interests have been eliminated, military strategy is more truly defensive against external aggressors and internal insurgency. Even in the twentieth century, small armies operating largely undercover with local support could frustrate the forces of the great powers, such as the Vietcong against the United States and the Afghani guerrillas against the Soviet Union; and this has become the model for military forces today. Britain, in common with most nations, employs a small, well-equipped military force, trained in the tactics of defensive warfare operating within their own territory; the strategy is to ensure that the damage that could be inflicted on an enemy far exceeds any benefit that such an enemy could hope to gain.

6 Religion

The withdrawal of religion

The parish church of All Saints has, over the nine hundred years since its foundation, presided over the building, decay and rebuilding of the cottages of Wickwyn several times over. For the first four hundred years of its existence, its priests were the moral guardians and spiritual pastors of the community, overlooking with undisputed authority every aspect of life. Although ordinary people – and the priests themselves – mostly fell far short of the ideals of Christian life, no one questioned the ultimate truth and value of those ideals. And this village church was part of the wider, Catholic Church which was called, so people believed, to give moral guidance to the social and political life of the whole of Christendom. All human thought and study was under the rule of the Church: theology was the queen of sciences, and those who wished to pursue higher learning travelled to monasteries and universities to study under the Church's watchful eye.

From its earliest centuries the Church felt at ease with the social order of the village. But the activities of merchants and traders evoked suspicion. Bishops and theologians warned of the spiritual dangers of buying and selling for profit. For a thousand years or more this was a matter of only minor concern, such trade being largely confined to the towns while the majority of people in the countryside were barely involved in the money economy. But in the late medieval period commerce began to expand rapidly, and increasing numbers of ordinary village people were engaged in making and supplying goods for trade. The theologians could no longer ignore this area of life, and their first response was to make rules to govern it. Merchants should pay a 'just price' to the producers, in proportion to the work involved in making the goods; and in selling goods the merchant should not exploit temporary shortages by raising prices. Usury – the charging of interest on loans – was outlawed and declared an anathema to divine commandment, punishable by excommunication or even death. Yet these rules were at most intended to prevent exploitation and anarchy as free trade expanded, rather than to make trade morally desirable. On the contrary, merchants were urged to make amends for their self-interested activity by giving generously to the Church, and much of the lavish church building of the late medieval period was financed by profits from trade.

Soon, however, the theologians' rules proved inadequate. As trade expanded, and as the methods of financing it became more complex, the theologians were forced constantly to revise and extend their rulings to give moral guidance to each new development. So eventually a God-fearing merchant, seeking to follow the Church's teaching, would have found himself paralysed by the weight of moral laws. Eventually the attempt was abandoned, and by the fifteenth century even usury was permissible. Thus, in the following centuries the Church withdrew from wider economic and social concerns, confining its moral teaching and pastoral care to personal and family matters. Religion and politics grew apart. The primary business of religion was seen as the inner spiritual salvation of the individual, while that of politics was the outward well-being of society – and the two spheres came to be regarded as quite separate.

By the Industrial Revolution of the early nineteenth century the divorce was complete. The captains of the new industries were frequently pillars of the church, and like the medieval merchants they gave generously to the building and restoration of churches. But their Christian allegiance did not constrain their pursuit of profit. Although many church people were deeply concerned at the poverty and degradation in the industrial cities, founding charities and pressing for legislation to alleviate it, the Church had no moral judgement to make on the political and economic system which caused the degradation. Theology – the knowledge of God – was no longer the queen of sciences, guiding all human study and understanding; it was regarded as a specialized field of inquiry and expertise, alongside other academic disciplines, to be acquired by the Church's ministers. The Church no longer incorporated every member of society, the majority of the working classes regarding it with indifference or even outright hostility as the pious gathering of

the wealthy. And ministers increasingly insisted on the importance of individual belief as the criterion of Church membership,
thus sharpening the division between the faithful Christian
assured of salvation and the rest of humanity.

In Wickwyn change came more slowly, but the same social
and spiritual forces were at work. Whereas in the industrial
cities of the nineteenth century the mass of working people no
longer had any connection with the Church, in the villages
squires and farm workers alike continued to attend Sunday
worship. But the enclosure of the parish, depriving the peasants
of their ancient rights and turning them into employees, fundamentally changed the social fabric of the village, which in turn
changed people's attitudes to the local church. It was no longer
the heart of the whole community, but was perceived as the
landowners' church to which others came out of deference or
simply habit. By the beginning of the twentieth century this
habit was visibly weakening, and attendance at Wickwyn
church was in steady decline. And in the years after the First
World War this decline became a slump. As the village population dwindled, so church-going fell even more rapidly; and as
church-going ceased to be part of the normal routine of village
life, so people no longer felt any obligation to attend. By the late
twentieth century regular attendance had fallen to a tiny handful of people, so committed that they were prepared to stand the
rigours of a cold and damp church in order to worship God.

Though physically the church still stood at the centre of the
village, it was now marginal to its life. As the few remaining
houses in the village were lavishly decorated and equipped by
the affluent farmers and commuters who inhabited them, the
church building gradually decayed. In a period of unprecedented material riches, the Church experienced unprecedented
poverty. Its own traditional sources of income, the rent from its
land and the dividends from its shares, could not keep pace
with salaries and wages. Thus, not only was there insufficient
cash to maintain the fabric, but also a parish priest for each
community could not be afforded. At the same time far fewer
people were offering themselves for ordination, and so clergy
numbers were rapidly reduced. By 1980, Wickwyn was one of a
group of eight small parishes served by a single priest. On
Sundays he was kept busy travelling from one sparsely attended

service to another; but on weekdays, with only just over a thousand souls in his parishes, he found himself with little to do. When asked, he readily complained of overwork, but in truth he was so uncertain of his role and purpose that even quite simple tasks seemed burdensome. He was relieved that many people still sought his services for weddings and funerals, but was inwardly hurt that at most times he was treated with benevolent disregard.

Parish worship

The clergy have always been prone to see church attendance as an index of their own success or failure; and so the dwindling of congregations throughout the twentieth century added to the clergy's burden of anxiety. But in fact the individual clergyman had little long-term effect. The decline of the Church was a symptom of the breakdown of the community which it served. Those religious groups which remained strong in the twentieth century depended on a sense of corporate social solidarity which found expression in worship – amongst black immigrants in inner cities, for example. For the parish church the task was to foster the same sense of solidarity within a local community, and to do so the Church's moral concern and spiritual care needed to reach out to every aspect of social and economic life. Then, in turn, people would want and need to express their commitment to one another in worship.

This is precisely what has happened in recent decades in villages such as Wickwyn, as the population has expanded and as people have looked to the local community to satisfy their material and emotional needs. They have come to see the church as the spiritual heart of the life they are establishing within the village, expressing their common identity and celebrating their common experiences. The firm boundary which the Church erected in the nineteenth and twentieth centuries between believer and non-believer has been gradually disappearing, and people with little or no doctrinal conviction, as well as those with firmly-held theological beliefs, find in the church support and encouragement. But, unlike the inhabitants of the medieval village, the newcomers do not share a uniform culture, but have a great variety of social backgrounds, including a minority of Hindus and Muslims whose ancestors came to Britain in the late twentieth century. The church must thus seek to reflect this pluriformity, and yet express the unity and identity of the community as a whole. It does this by combining a deep respect for the old traditions of English Christianity with an openness to fresh insights and ideas, so that the traditions continue to live and to develop in response to the present situation.

The climaxes of the church's life are the great festivals, which draw together the whole community of Wickwyn. The three main Christian festivals, of Christmas, Easter and Pentecost, celebrate the three basic spiritual aspects of human life, love, hope and faith. A pine tree has been planted on the village green near the churchyard, and at Christmas this is decorated with lights and stars: at eleven o'clock on Christmas Eve great crowds gather round to sing carols, accompanied by the village band, and to celebrate the perfect love represented by the coming of the God-man to share human existence; then the people process into the church for Communion. At Easter, as night falls, the people meet outside the church, where a large paschal candle is lit, and each person lights his own small candle from it, representing the hope that wherever there is darkness and despair in people's lives new light can come; then, as at Christmas, the people process into the church, singing an Easter hymn, to celebrate Communion. And at Pentecost, again on the village green, a great fire is lit to symbolize God's Spirit reaching out to each person to unite them in loyalty and faith; hymns are sung and Communion is celebrated in the open air, after which a feast is cooked on the fire. Even those who come to church only at these major festivals are happy to receive Communion, since the attitude which grew up after the Reformation, that the sacrament was only for the most committed Christians, has gone. Now the eating of the bread and wine is seen as a celebration of the corporate life of the whole community, rather than the private devotion of the religious individual; and infants and children are also invited to share in it, since they are equal members of the community.

In addition to the Christian festivals, the Hindu festival of Diwali in late October, and the Muslim festival of Eid to mark

74

the end of their annual fast, have been to some degree adopted by the whole village. At Diwali it is not only Hindus, but almost every household, that put a lamp in their front window, symbolizing, like the candles of Easter, the triumph of light over darkness; and small presents of sweets and cakes are exchanged. At Eid, the Muslims not only celebrate within their own families, but they hold a great feast in the village hall to which all are invited.

The church also marks four other festivals which, although traditional to English Christianity, do not originate in the Christian story, but which in varying forms can be found in most religions. In May there is Rogation, when people walk round the parish boundary asking God's blessing on the crops in the fields and on the work of the village. Although there is a solemn intention, the atmosphere is like that of a summer outing, and people bring picnic lunches to eat on the way. In early October there is Harvest Thanksgiving, when the church is decorated not only with fruit and vegetables but also with various goods made in the village, such as furniture, toys, bricks – and even a sample of the synthetic material made in the factory. In early November, the old festivals of All Saints and of Remembrance Day have been brought together as a single memorial for loved ones who have died; in the small side chapel of the church, where a book is kept recording the names of the dead, people place candles, and there is a simple service of remembrance. In March, the old tradition of Mothering Sunday is kept, when children give spring flowers to their mothers; during the service parents, spouses and children in turn say a prayer, renewing their commitment to their families.

The church has inaugurated one new festival, a Covenant Service held in late August, marking the beginning of the church's calendar. This has been developed partly from a Methodist tradition and partly from the ancient liturgy for Easter. During the service people renew their baptismal vows as followers of Christ, and water from the font is sprinkled on the congregation. Of all the festivals it has the most exclusively Christian connotation, and is attended only by those in the village who regard themselves as convinced Christians, coming to worship Sunday by Sunday.

A person from the late twentieth century visiting the ordinary Sunday worship of the church would be surprised at its old-fashioned flavour. While the festivals often attract up to two hundred people, the congregation on a normal Sunday is rarely more than fifty, which is about 5 per cent of the population. Most of the newcomers have little or no Christian background, so the old barriers between Catholic, Anglican and Nonconformist do not apply, and all Christians are happy to worship together. The basic shape of the service is that of the Roman Catholic rite that was composed in the mid-twentieth century, but many of the traditional prayers from the Book of Common Prayer, written in the sixteenth century and used in Wickwyn for five centuries, have been incorporated. Yet at the same time, within this firm framework there is a high degree of freedom and spontaneity, with different styles of music used, with children performing short dramas, and with a time of free prayer in which members of the congregation offer prayers as they feel moved; thus the atmosphere is relaxed and informal. Communion is celebrated each week, and for the central part of the service the congregation stands in a circle in the chancel, which has been cleared of all furniture; the Communion table, made in the early seventeenth century, is placed in the middle, and the bread and wine passed from one person to another. They have thus revived the practice of the English reformers who wanted to emphasize that the Communion is a celebration of people's fellowship. The attitude of the congregation, although it is a minority within the village, is not that of an exclusive group regarding itself as superior to those who come to worship only occasionally at festivals; rather they see themselves as privileged in the enjoyment and strength they receive from regular worship, and are willing to arrange festival worship on behalf of the whole community.

Just as the ancient festivals now have new life and meaning, so also do the rites of passage. Whereas by the late twentieth century it was a dying custom, most parents now bring their infants for baptism as, regardless of their precise religious conviction, they want themselves and their children to be formally part of the spiritual, as well as the social and economic, life of the village. And to emphasize that infants and children are full members of the community, they are given the bread and the wine of Communion as soon as they are baptized. Church weddings, too, had become less common in the twentieth century, but again within Wickwyn the great majority of marriages now take place in church; and even the Hindus and Muslims often have part of their own ceremonies there. The trend that started in the twentieth century of couples living together before marriage has now become well accepted as normal and sensible. Couples generally have an engagement party, after which they set up home together for a trial period, usually of one or two years, during which they do not have children. Then, usually in late spring or summer, they have the wedding ceremony in church, to mark their lifelong commitment to one another. Homosexual couples can also now take marriage vows in church, so that they are bound by the same moral expectations of lifelong fidelity as heterosexual couples. And although some continue to feel uneasy and privately disapproving of homosexuality, publicly homosexual marriage is now openly acceptable, and is seen to have the same spiritual and emotional value as heterosexual marriage.

Even at the nadir of religious observance in the twentieth century, most continued to want a Christian funeral. But the factory-like atmosphere of many crematoria in which most funerals took place reflected the prevailing attitude to death: it was seen simply as the end of life, the point where the physical body had become useless and so had to be disposed of in the most efficient way possible. Now the great majority wish their dead to be buried in the churchyard. The greater sense of community means that people no longer regard life as belonging only to individuals, but to groups also, in particular the family and the village; thus the dead, in both the mystical religious sense of eternal life, and in the emotional sense of their memory being treasured by those close to them, remain unified with their loved ones – and this is symbolized by burial in the parish churchyard. Paradoxically, this greater sense of community has an additional effect which prevents the churchyard from becoming too full for further burials. The fashion for permanent stone memorials, which developed in the late eighteenth and nineteenth centuries, reflected a transition from traditional religious belief to a secular individualistic attitude to death; people wished to preserve outwardly the memory of their loved ones as a bulwark against the growing attitude to death merely as extinction. Now people are happy to return to the old custom of burying their dead in a shroud or simple coffin that will decompose with the body itself, and to have no outward memorial, so that the churchyard can be redug as often as every twenty or thirty years. The conduct of the funeral service itself has become more personal and intimate, with friends rather than paid pallbearers carrying the body to the grave.

The medieval Church had been organized as a rigid hierarchy, with bishops and priests dispensing sacraments and guidance to an obedient flock; and in this they reflected the stable hierarchical ordering of society as a whole. The Church in industrial society remained hierarchical, with the professional clergyman ministering to a passive people, but for the opposite reason. In a world in which the individual was alone responsible for his or her own destiny, the Church, for those who attended it, offered an antidote through which people could feel secure and safe. In the village of today, in which people both exercise a high degree of individual responsibility for their lives and yet belong to a stable and supportive community, every member of the congregation is now regarded as sharing the Church's ministry. No longer does the Church need to give implicit sanction to the existing social order, nor provide an escape from it; but rather through the Church people can give mutual encouragement and guidance in the challenges and difficulties they face in their daily lives.

This new understanding of church life is reflected in the pattern of ministry which, without conscious intention, is akin to that envisioned by John Wesley three hundred years ago, whose view of church life closely resembles what has now evolved. There are a number of local priests – like Wesley's local preachers – who have charge of the worship of the church and who organize study groups. There are local pastors – like Wesley's class-leaders – who each have assigned to them one part of the village, where they both visit the sick and, if they gain the respect and trust of people, are turned to as advisers and counsellors. And there is a group of churchwardens – like Wesley's stewards – who have charge of the material resources of the church, including the church building itself. The vicar, who is the only person who is paid to work full-time for the church, is thus no longer required to run its daily life; his role is much closer to that of the apostles of the early Church – and of Wesley's ministers – acting as 'spiritual ambassadors' linking the local parish with the wider Church. The fall in clergy numbers and financial resources in the twentieth century, which forced Wickwyn to become part of a group of eight parishes with a single vicar, has proved appropriate for this new pattern of ministry. His task is to guide and support the local priests, pastors and wardens, as well as sharing with them in preaching and caring for people. He travels widely, not only between his parishes but far beyond, often visiting churches in other parts of the country to preach and to gain fresh insights to bring back to his own parishes.

As in the medieval village, the Church is again at the heart of the local community. Yet, as in the industrial age, there is a wide diversity of religious beliefs and attitudes, with the Church's priests and theologians no longer credited with a monopoly of truth. Thus the number of regular worshippers remains a small proportion of the population; but the majority celebrate the festivals and rites of passage in church and, even if they do not share its theology, they feel at one with the moral and social values for which the Church stands. The life and ministry of the Church is like that of Jesus Christ and his followers: there is a small, strong centre of committed disciples and a wide soft edge of people who look to the Church for support and strength at the important times of their lives.

Parish art

Over the centuries the building, decorating and furnishing of Wickwyn parish church, like most village churches, involved some of the finest craftsmanship and art of which man is capable. The original small rectangular church built in Norman times – perhaps using some of the Saxon masonry of an earlier building – is now virtually hidden by later additions, apart from the simple rounded arch, with zigzag carving, of the south door. The two aisles, with arched windows and stone tracery forming a series of interlocking Y shapes, were built in the thirteenth century; and a hundred years later a south chapel was added with a magnificent perpendicular window through which the sun casts delicate shadows on the floor below. The tower and spire were built in the early seventeenth century to house a peal of four bells. In medieval times every wall and pillar had been decorated with murals illustrating the Bible stories and the lives of the saints, including a picture of St Christopher on the wall opposite the south door, so that people on their way to the fields or on a journey could briefly look in and ask him to pray for their safety. On the huge wooden roof beams are carved angels, bunches of flowers and leaves; and outside the church are stone gargoyles carved with grotesque faces and bodies, perhaps caricaturing unpopular local dignitaries.

The church was the focus of the artistic life of the community. The murals were the main means through which people learnt the Christian stories which embedded themselves in the popular imagination. Occasionally groups of travelling players would appear in the village, and perform religious drama in the church. Music, too, was largely bound up with church worship, and in the fifteenth century a rood-screen was constructed across the chancel arch, on which perched a small choir and orchestra. So, through architecture, painting, drama and music the church conveyed from one generation to the next the spiritual and moral values on which the community was founded.

But the Reformation brought radical change. The reformers themselves were suspicious of all forms of religious art as idolatrous, standing in the way of people's direct relationship with God. The walls were therefore whitewashed and the stone pillars scrubbed to remove the paintings; statues of the saints were removed, and all that remained were the wall brackets on which they stood; and the only music that was permitted was the deadly monotony of the metrical psalms, with the parish clerk shouting out a verse, and the congregation shouting it back. Art was thus forced out of the religious and into the secular world, and the role of artists changed accordingly. No longer did they have a particular purpose and function, to express Christian values through symbol and image, but their task was simply to express their own individual vision, and if possible find a patron or market for their work. Thus the individualism of economic, social and religious life pervaded art also. And just as economic individualism brought spectacular material progress, so artistic individualism produced works of exquisite beauty and soaring imagination, as artists were freed from the demands and conventions of the Church. The eighteenth and nineteenth centuries saw a flowering of painting, music, poetry and novel-writing. During this period artists often replaced the discipline of the Church by consciously creating 'schools' or 'movements', such as the impressionist painters of the late nineteenth century or the romantic poets of a few decades earlier; or by establishing strict forms in which to work, such as the sonata form in music, or the geometrical rules of neo-classical architecture. But these schools and rules had no binding force on artists, who were always free to experiment with new forms and ideas.

In the twentieth century, however, the artistic world became increasingly fragmented, and the self-imposed disciplines virtually disappeared, leaving artists total and bewildering freedom. It ceased to be possible to discern trends or movements, but instead there was a multiplicity of small groups and individuals each pursuing their own particular line. Serious music degenerated into esoteric experiments into different patterns of sounds; and the invention of the sound synthesizer meant that even the material discipline imposed by the nature of the musical instruments themselves no longer applied. In the visual arts the photograph took away from painting the one social function it continued to have, that of portraying people and places, and so painters were left to abstract from external reality the underlying forms and colours that they perceived. In architecture the widespread use of reinforced concrete meant that the shapes of buildings were no longer determined by the physical limitations of the materials themselves, so architects could, like painters, create such forms as their imagination invented. Poetry, which had originated with popular verses and ballads handed on by word of mouth, was now the narrow preserve of a literary circle in which writers experimented with words as composers did with sounds.

By the late twentieth century serious art of all kinds had become separated not only from religious life but also from the understanding and imagination of ordinary people. This vacuum was filled by the prolific output of the electronic media – radio, television and the recording studio – satisfying popular taste with music and drama that was expertly produced and pleasurable to hear and see, but which had no role or purpose beyond immediate entertainment. At the same time there was a deep nostalgia for the past, a yearning for the stability and cohesion that history seemed to represent. Churches, in common with many other old buildings, became the objects of public attention and money to conserve them as memorials of the past. And in the last two decades of the twentieth century there was a reaction against the weird and jarring shapes of modern concrete architecture, and a self-conscious return to soft red brick and steep-pitched, tiled roofs. Popular music was constantly raiding the past to revive old styles, and popular films were frequently set in bygone ages when manners were more delicate and the landscape more gentle.

Today artists are again at the centre of society, the channel through which people's hopes and values, their anxieties and fears, find expression. The technical and imaginative freedom which artists had come to enjoy is preserved, and they are not bound either by ecclesiastical conventions or by the arbitrary rules of some school or movement. But, like medieval artists, their role in society puts them under a spiritual and moral discipline because, if they are to find acceptance and respect, their work must respond and speak to the community in which they exist.

Wickwyn's church is a focus of artistic creativity. In the aisles a local artist has painted four large panels showing four of Christ's images of the Kingdom of God, using people and scenes from Wickwyn in the pictures: the sower sowing a field; the man building a house on firm foundations; the good shepherd tending sheep; and a woman mixing yeast in dough. In the south chapel another local artist has pictured the creation, with animals, birds and plants that can be found in the countryside round the village. There is a church orchestra, with flutes and violins, guitars and tambourines, to lead the music at services, especially the festivals; and they often use songs and settings of the Communion composed by members of the orchestra itself. The preachers in church rarely give the kind of dry theological sermon which the Reformation had encouraged, and which even in the twentieth century was the norm; instead, as with Jesus himself, the gift of preaching lies in telling stories and describing scenes which grip the imagination, and which can be used to express and explain the gospel. A church drama group writes and enacts short plays to be used during services, or longer productions to fill the whole evening; these, like the medieval religious plays, deal with the deepest mysteries of human life in a way which is vivid and accessible to the popular imagination.

Unlike medieval society, however, the church does not have a monopoly of the creative arts. The greater prosperity and freedom of modern life allows far more time and energy for artistic endeavour; and the greater moral and spiritual importance both of the family and of the local community means that ordinary homes and the village itself can be objects of the same aesthetic care as the church. A large proportion of people have creative gifts of some kind, and so many devote a number of hours each week, in addition to their normal work, to developing and using these gifts. There is thus within the village a flourishing exchange of artistic objects and services, with people selling their work at little more than their direct expenses. So most homes, and the hospital and school, have original pictures hanging on the wall and sculptures on mantelpieces and windowsills. There are frequent concerts, exhibitions and plays at the village hall. Many of the individual gardens, as well as a garden in one corner of the village green and another adjacent to the village hall, are beautifully laid out, their shrubberies designed with graceful elegance. As in the past, architecture is now constrained by material and technical needs, and the requirements of energy efficiency combined with the cheapness of local bricks mean that the new buildings have the same gentle simplicity as those of ancient Wickwyn.

There is inevitably a degree of crudeness in much of the local art, and if the village were isolated from the outside world the artistic imagination would become sterile. But television and radio provide daily contact with the wider world and many people visit Peterthorpe to see professional concerts and plays, so that local art is stimulated and its standards raised by the creative genius of great writers, painters and performers. At the same time, this creative genius is itself profoundly influenced by the renewal of local art. The debilitating lack of meaning and purpose that infected all forms of art in the nineteenth and twentieth centuries has now been cured by the conviction shared by artists at all levels that their work is vital to the moral and spiritual health of the society which they serve.

Community and ideology

Three miles to the south-east of Wickwyn, at Hymen Parva, a monastery was established in the eleventh century. At its height it housed over forty monks, and attracted many young people to be educated there. It followed the Benedictine Rule, where worship, study and manual work were all part of the monks' daily life, and where the humblest tasks were regarded as part of divine worship: as Benedict expressed it, the ordinary cooking pots and tools of the monastery should be regarded 'as if they were the sacred vessels of the altar'. In small ways it often experimented in new techniques of agriculture, stimulating local peasant farmers to imitate them and so improve their crops. Through its way of life it was a focus for the Christian vision and ideal, and in common with many monasteries it helped to permeate an often brutal and violent culture with Christian values. Sadly, in later medieval times it grew wealthy and corrupt, and became a burden on the economy and the spirit of the locality, so that when it was dissolved in the sixteenth century there was little regret.

In the seventeenth century, shortly before the Civil War, another Christian Community was founded at Hymen Parva. It was based on a single extended family, with two brothers and a sister with their respective spouses and children sharing a large manor house; in addition there were a number of single people, including four elderly widows cared for by the Community. Its pattern of worship was based on the Book of Common Prayer drawn up by the English reformers, with morning and evening prayer being said daily in a small chapel; in this they were indirectly inspired by the monastic vision, since the reformers had condensed the old monastic offices into two services, in the hope that the life of corporate prayer would no longer be confined to monks and nuns but shared by ordinary families. Like the monks, they worked a small farm and had various crafts. And they, too, worked and prayed for the society in which they lived, that the seeds of the gospel would grow and bear fruit in the world of politics and commerce. But now the ground was more stony and less fertile, for the economic and political changes which brought about the Industrial Revolution were already in evidence. The Civil War itself was the first major political landmark in this change, and the Community at Hymen Parva, which briefly harboured the defeated King shortly before his capture, was ransacked by marauding parliamentary soldiers.

Three-and-a-half centuries later, in the early 1980s, a third religious Community was started at Hymen Parva, comprising a number of families and single people from various social backgrounds and Christian traditions. Like the monastery of medieval times, it was one of a number of similar Communities which sprang up in the late twentieth and twenty-first centuries. When it started, its values and way of life were seemingly at odds with those of society as a whole, and its members were often accused of being Utopian and escapist. But since then the millions who have come to repopulate the countryside of Britain have followed a similar path, aspiring to similar values; and now the Community at Hymen Parva is an integral and harmonious part of the local scene.

Its way of life is outwardly very similar to that of the surrounding villages, but incorporating in a more full-blooded way the ethos on which village life depends. As in the village, each family has its own house, they cultivate a small garden and farm, and they have a number of workshops where members produce a variety of different goods. But the land and the buildings are held in common, so that the members must co-operate closely in their daily work. Twice a week the whole Community gathers to share a meal. Major policy decisions are made by the whole Community seeking unanimity, so that the views of each person have to be listened to and there is no scope for the formation of factions within the Community. Each morning the Community meets for a simple act of worship, and on Saturday evening has its own informal celebration of Communion, so that on Sunday morning the members can attend local parish churches, including that at Wickwyn.

In the monastery the ordinary monk did not claim for himself any exceptional holiness or goodness, but it was through his vocation as part of the Community that he bore witness to the gospel. Similarly, the people at Hymen Parva are not exceptional or special, yet together play an important social and spiritual role: while to the members themselves the Community is simply a satisfying and fulfilling way of life to which they feel called, to those outside it can serve as a place of learning and of healing. Each year four or five people, mostly young but some in middle or old age, come to live at Hymen Parva to share in the life of the Community and to study various aspects of Christian faith and practice; within the Community there are four members expert in different fields of learning who supervise this study, and there is a library well stocked in these fields. The Community also welcomes people to stay for short periods to reflect privately, or to recover from personal difficulties: through sharing in the Community's daily life, and through the friendships which grow with its members, many whose self-respect is low and whose lives seem dark and lonely, find spiritual and emotional refreshment.

The Community at Hymen Parva in its life and purpose thus complements the solid core of church members in the surrounding parishes such as Wickwyn. In both there is a conscious commitment to follow the teaching of the gospel in every aspect of life. In Wickwyn it is done in the context of an ordinary village, so that while the influence on the life of the village may be great, it is largely hidden and its source is not obvious. The overt influence of Hymen Parva is negligible because it is set apart, but precisely for this reason the ideals of Christianity are more clearly focused in its pattern of life.

Epilogue: Theology

The sacramental society

Five centuries ago a ruling went out that in every parish church above the Communion table there should be inscribed the Ten Commandments, the Apostles' Creed and the Lord's Prayer. And so great oak panels, on which were written these bold statements of faith, were placed on the east wall of Wickwyn church. At the time theology, 'the science of God', was still the queen of sciences, and people saw the whole universe as ruled by the divine will: thus the task of the theologian and preacher was to define as precisely as possible the nature of God and his dealings with mankind; and the laity were required to believe and do as they were told. And this divine rule was, people assumed, embodied in the structures of society itself: that the strict and stable order of village life, each person with their time-honoured duties and rights, was ordained by God.

But already, even as the oak boards were erected, the Reformation, and the social and economic changes which it presaged, were beginning to make the throne of theology less secure; it was as if the Church, dimly aware of these changes, reacted by asserting its authority more forcefully. One hundred and fifty years later, in the eighteenth century, the wooden brackets on which the boards hung rotted, and the boards fell to the ground; they were taken into the vestry where they remain to this day. Outside the church, the village was at the start of a process of change which was to relegate the Church to a position of virtual irrelevance, in a world where economic growth was the new god. The stable, unchanging social order was replaced by a new order in which individual choice and the pursuit of material gain were the mainsprings of society, and where there was continuous progress and change.

Now, on the east wall of Wickwyn church behind the Communion table, a new wooden panel has been erected, on which is written in simple fawn lettering on a cream background, the famous words of St Paul: 'Faith, hope and love abide, these three, and the greatest of these is love.' These words express a simple creed to which almost everyone, however diverse their other beliefs, can give assent, for they come not from metaphysical speculation but from actual human experience. In modern Wickwyn theology does not rule, but nor does the god of material prosperity. Rather, the basic values on which society depends consist in the fusion of the spiritual and the material, the personal and the economic: through working together at an economic level and sharing common material concerns, people in the community can grow together in spirit; economic relationships being the means through which personal relationships develop and deepen. Wickwyn, like any community of people, can be riven by the petty jealousies and selfishness to which all human hearts are prone. But the daily life and work of the community is anxious to encourage rather than prevent personal relationships, and so create the channels through which people can be drawn together in love and mutual care.

If growth in love is the primary purpose of human life, then faith is the soil within which it takes root. In modern Wickwyn the individual is not bound by social obligation, nor is the free will of the individual supreme; rather, individuals are free to order their own lives within a strong framework of personal and social commitments. This interplay of the individual and the corporate will is the outward expression of the inner quality of faith. Within the family, amongst friends, and in the community as a whole, faithfulness consists in constantly seeking to listen and respond to the feelings and attitudes of others, even when there is tension and discord. There are innumerable instances in Wickwyn, as in any community, when faith is damaged or broken, when rifts or divisions are created because people are too stubborn and too prejudiced to try to understand those with whom they disagree. Yet the social structure itself, in which individuals exercise a high degree of control over their own lives, and yet depend on the co-operation and the goodwill of others, means that only through an attitude of faith and mutual trust can people flourish and prosper.

In the human soul there is both the desire for stability and security, and at the same time a yearning for progress and change. At various times in history, and in various societies, one or other of these predominates; and both can readily find religious justification, since the stable order can be interpreted as reflecting the unchanging divine order, and progress can be seen as the unfolding of God's will guiding mankind towards its ultimate fulfilment. Modern society, however, has neither the stultifying stability of the medieval village nor the unbridled compulsion for change of high capitalism, but is simultaneously both conservative and radical. The re-emergence of a sense of community requires time for common traditions and patterns of behaviour to develop in which people feel secure and confident; yet individual freedom implies that those with energy and ambition will bring change, in which old ideas and ways are questioned, and fresh approaches are adopted.

When the Holy Communion was celebrated in Wickwyn church in medieval times, the service took place behind the rood-screen, with the priest and his acolytes at the altar performing elaborate and complex rituals, while the ordinary people standing in the nave were able to see little and understand nothing. This form of worship reflected a theology and a society in which the spiritual realm represented by the priestly rituals dominated the daily material lives of ordinary people; the corporate will, expressed in the moral teaching of the Church, dominated the individual will; and the forces of stability overwhelmed the forces of change. By the eighteenth and nineteenth centuries Communion had ceased to be celebrated, except at occasional services attended by only a handful of pious souls for whom the sacrament was an aid to their private devotions; and religion itself was seen by the majority as irrelevant, a spare-time hobby enjoyed by a diminishing minority. This reflected an era in which the material realm had come to dominate the spiritual, leaving little place for religion; the individual will was stronger than any moral or social obligation; and people believed that humankind was capable of limitless progress in its quest to control the natural order for its own ends.

In the second half of the twentieth century the Churches began to celebrate Communion in a way that foreshadowed, in symbol and ritual, the social changes that were to occur in the future. Christians wanted to celebrate Communion each week, with the whole congregation participating. People began to lead different parts of the service according to their ability; the hymns and songs became brighter and more tuneful; lay people brought the bread and the wine up to the Lord's Table; and, most of all, everyone received the sacraments. The bread and the wine are symbols of the fruits of human work, and in offering, consecrating and consuming them together people are celebrating a community in which production and consumption are sacramental: through working together and through sharing the fruits of that work, man's deepest spiritual needs are satisfied also. The social order that is emerging in the twenty-first century is sacramental in its values, its structures and its aspirations. It is a society in which, whether or not they regard themselves as religious, people can through the course of their daily lives find fulfilment both in body and in spirit; and so come to experience personally something of that which Christians call God.